ME, MYSELF AND WHO?

HUMANISM:
SOCIETY'S FALSE PREMISE

Ernest Gordon
Author of "Through the Valley of the Kwai"

Logos International
Plainfield, New Jersey

All Scripture references are taken from the King James
Version unless otherwise noted as RSV (Revised Standard
Version), NEB (The New English Bible), or TEV (Today's English
Version).

For Alastair—in
appreciation of a friendship
that has spanned twenty-eight
years.

Preface

The main problem of our time is not simply a shortage of fossil fuels, but essentially a shortage of spiritual energy. We have masses of data, and the means for physical analysis, but there is a shortage of metaphysical principles essential for understanding their coherence and purpose. We know how to put people on the moon, but we are short of means that will enable us to keep our cities clean of garbage, corruption and crime. Our universities are storehouses of knowledge, yet they lack the moral energy to integrate this knowledge and become moral communities. Children who have everything physically are dying of neglect.

Some may say the answer is more faith. Yet there is plenty of faith *qua* faith. Cults prosper even if conventional religious organizations wither away. Faith is common. Everyone has faith; that is, the ability to give his or her loyalty and devotion to some person, cause, ideology, party, nation or deity. The problem is not faith in itself. The problem comes when faith is given to the wrong object or cause.

My purpose in writing this book is to show it is the object of our faith that determines the quality and nature of our faith. Too much faith is placed in too many wrong objects and too little faith is placed in the Father of Jesus Christ who alone has proved himself worthy of our faith. The worthiness of His faith in us authenticates our faith in Him.

Contents

ME, MYSELF AND WHO?

1

The Faith That Fails

We all live by faith.

A recent graduate of Princeton University came to my study to tell me there was no place for me or the Christian faith on the campus. He told me this with a smile on his face. It was a smile of confidence. I use the word "confidence" advisedly, for "confidence" means "with faith." Patiently, I listened to his reasons for my proposed abolition. They seemed very old-fashioned to my ears, probably because I had heard them so often.

I shall sum up his position briefly:

1. It is absurd to believe in God. Faith such as mine is a superstition left over from the past. It is as useful in today's world as the appendix is to our bodies. The need for God has been done away with by the discoveries of science and the practice of psychiatry.

2. No longer is it necessary to think that religion is the basis of morality. Education has replaced the church and prayer and the Bible and the sacraments. A "better morality" is now being shaped—one that is non-judgmental. When Christianity is eradicated, the new-and-better morality will flourish.

3. People who believe as he does are the new

1

leaders. For the sake of those less educated than themselves, they have the responsibility of knocking over the idols of religion and tearing down the structures of the Christian faith.

His smile remained fixed as he poured out his belief for my edification. When his pace slowed down, I said to him, "You are a man of great faith, but I regret to inform you it is the *wrong* faith. I'll even go further to say it is satanic." A look of anger and disapproval suddenly replaced his smile.

"I have nothing to do with faith," was his rejoinder. "That is what I came to tell you. There is no room for faith on the campus. The sooner you realize it, the better."

I reminded him he was arguing from unexamined premises, and making statements he could not verify by any scientific method. He did not like my criticism. He soon left. On his way out of my office, he turned around in the doorway to make one last defense of his position: "I might have known I was only wasting my time talking to you!"

I report this incident as an illustration of the unrecognized and unadmitted faith that dominates the minds of many people on campuses. Like my visitor, they do not believe it is a form of faith. They are convinced it is knowledge intrinsic to them as intellectual human beings. Rather, it is faith without revelation.

It is this faith, therefore, that dominates the moods and manners of today's campuses. I would not attempt to deny its attractiveness, for it is appealing to most of us to believe we are completely autonomous. The appeal, however, may be only confined to youth, and then only for a fleeting moment, for the facts of existence teach us differently and, usually, very quickly. While cynicism in youth may be amusing, it is boring in middle age, and in old age it is pathetic.

This faith in man and in his institutions may be traced back to the Tower of Babel. The "Babel" is Hebrew for Babylon, meaning "gate of God."

In ancient times man expressed his faith as polytheism. The Tower of Babel exemplifies this. In the Sumero-Babylonian period we presume that the people built great *ziggurats*, or man-made mountains, to indicate their ability to control or manage the ultimate mystery whom we name God. Idols represented the various divine attributes. These idols were placed on the man-made towers, or ziggurats, according to their degrees of importance. Thus, the most important idol was elevated to the highest point. It may be that we have inherited the preposition "up," in referring to God's location, from this practice.

Such a way of managing God suited the purposes of rulers. These rulers encouraged their subjects to think of them as divine, and to deify their attributes in terms suitable to the purposes of the state. This is something that city-states, kingdoms, empires and civilizations have always done. Their idols invariably refer to power, laws, communication, pleasure, unity and so on. Man-made religion invariably repressed, suppressed, frustrated, confused and alienated individuals in their search for God.

The Israelites were those who responded to God's revelation; therefore, it is understandable why they should have been so shocked by the building of the Tower of Babel. Its destruction was seen by them clearly as an act of God. We may, if we choose, see the Tower of Babel as the prototype of the secular city or civilization. What is this but the manufactured technocracy in which God is rejected, and things and techniques are deemed to be more valuable than individual people. I think it is important to remember the conclusion of the biblical story. "Therefore is the name of it called Babel; because the Lord did there confound the language of all the earth; and from thence did the Lord scatter them abroad upon the face of all the earth" (Gen. 11:9).

Nowhere has the distaste for this man-centered faith been so brilliantly displayed than in these splendid words of Isaiah:

> To whom then will ye liken God?
> or what likeness will ye compare unto him?
> The workman melteth a graven image,
> and the goldsmith spreadeth it over with gold,
> and casteth silver chains.
> He that is so impoverished that he hath no oblation
> chooseth a tree that will not rot;
> he seeketh unto him a cunning workman
> to prepare a graven image. (Isa. 40:18-20)

Here the prophet shows us the poverty, the emptiness, the futility of a godless existence. Such existence is the highest form of stupidity as the Psalmist tells us, "The fool hath said in his heart, there is no God" (Ps. 14:1).

If we regard this situation as bad in the light of the prophet's and the Psalmist's condemnation, then how much worse is our contemporary situation?

We know better.
We have the Bible.
We have the witness of God's people.
We have the fullness of the divine revelation in Jesus Christ.
We have the benefits of Christianized civilization,

4

which include a reasonable morality, a personal style of living, just laws, means of education, high forms of cultural expression in all the arts; and science—our knowledge of the physical world and its laws.

We, who have so much, have the greater responsibility. "For unto whomsoever much is given, of him shall be much required" (Luke 12:48). Thus, if fault is to be attributed to those before Christ, how much more must fault be attributed, in these days, to those who will not travel in God's way of holiness, nor walk with His Son whose invitation is always most gracious, "Come unto me, all ye that labor, and are heavy laden, and I will give you rest" (Matt. 11:28).

If the waiting world in the days before Christ was pagan, it was still a world created and sustained by God. G.K. Chesterton has pointed out in *The Everlasting Man* that human beings are always taller when they kneel to pray, and always more dignified when they stoop to serve. He states that monotheism preceded polytheism. The tragedy of human beings, and the evidence of the Fall, is that the awareness of the *one*, holy God was too big for small human minds. They preferred to create idols in their own image.

The amazing growth and widespread outreach of early Christianity demonstrates that the pagan world was one in which people had a God-shaped emptiness that only God could fill through Jesus Christ.

The coming of Christ, therefore, has initiated judgment. In this judgment our present civilization is involved. Perhaps the horrors related in our daily news are evidences of this judgment.

T.S. Eliot deals with this theme in *Choruses from the Rock*. In the past, he tells us, people left God for other gods. Now people turn from God to "no-gods." He then goes on to list these "no-gods": "the grandeur of your mind," "the glory of your action," "schemes of human greatness," "devising the perfect refrigerator," "plotting of happiness," "humanity," "race." This list gives an honest description of the man-centered faith that goes by the name of *humanism.* Later on we shall discuss the many expressions of this substitute faith, and its domination of Western civilizations and Western universities.

The uniqueness of the Christian faith.

As Christians we affirm that our faith is centered upon Jesus Christ who is God's personal revelation: "the Word was made flesh." St. John tells us, he "dwelt among us, (and we beheld his glory, the glory as of the only begotten of the Father) full of grace and truth" (John 1:14).

The living God, therefore, has initiated this faith by His deliberate unveiling of himself. When we speak of revelation, we seem to be speaking in paradoxical terms; for revelation implies, first of all, hiddenness. This is the aspect of mystery declared by the Psalmist, "He made darkness his secret place; his pavilion round about him were dark waters and thick clouds of the skies" (Ps. 18:11). And the Psalmist is correct.

We cannot prove God as we may prove a financial account, or a sum in arithmetic, or a formula in chemistry. If we can prove anything at all, it is only that which is less than us, never that which is more than us. Neither can we ascend to God in the manner of the Sumero-Babylonians, nor by means of reason or secret knowledge. Thus God in His own nature is the ultimate mystery beyond the reach of our intelligence. *But*— and this "but" makes all the difference—although we

6

cannot go to God under our own steam, God has come to us. He has come to us in the only way we can understand—in the flesh. The flesh is our level. At this level He has addressed us. He has made His home with us that we may be at home with Him.

It is in the flesh that we begin our pilgrimage with, and unto, God. But only because He has come to us as our Elder Brother, and Companion/Teacher. When St. Peter answered the great question of Jesus about His identity, and said, "Thou art the Christ, the Son of the living God"; Jesus replied, "Blessed art thou, Simon Barjona: for flesh and blood hath not revealed it unto thee, but my Father which is in heaven" (Matt. 16:16, 17). In a similar vein St. Paul reminds us "that no man can say that Jesus is the Lord, but by the Holy Ghost" (1 Cor. 12:3).

Although people were aware of God, nevertheless they could not be fully aware until God revealed His mystery. And behold, this mystery was seen to have a human face. On the face—the face of our Lord—is a welcoming smile. Why, we may ask, has God chosen to do this? The answer is given clearly in John 3:16: "For God so loved the world, that He gave his only begotten Son, that whosoever believeth in him should not perish but have everlasting life."

The faith that is centered upon Jesus as Lord is affirmative. It affirms the world as God's. It affirms the nature, extent and range of His love. It affirms the glory and triumph of the life God gives us. It affirms each one of us, and thereby grants us our uniqueness and identity.

A close study of the history of the secular faith we call *humanism*, shows us that it negates human life and all that, in its beginning, it claims to be upholding. It was the emptiness of this lifeless faith that formed the background of my own experience.

In the years before World War II, I had been influenced by the intellectual climate, which was one of rationalistic optimism—the belief that mankind could create Utopia through the benefits of human reason, the methods of the positive sciences and the miracles of technology. Not everyone at universities believed this, but this was the faith that was touted by the press, the politicians and the media.

Then came World War II. From the campus I went to the battlefield, and then to the infamous Japanese prison camps on the Railroad of Death in Thailand. In such a situation there was no room for humanism. The war itself declared the death-affirming qualities of this faith in its ruthless disregard of God's commands. Germany was a technocracy that claimed the right to rule the world in its own way. The Nazis were merely its mad slaves. Technocracy and the belief in the superman, the hero-god, and the fictitious super-race of Aryans, controlled the mind of Germany and led to a desperate and bloody struggle. People like myself who were in the struggle hoped we were fighting for the freedom of people.

I had been in Germany as a schoolboy in 1934, and had been shocked by the ruthlessness of the Nazis. The German people were trained to be a brutal machine, each individual being nothing more than a wheel or a cog. The alternative to this mechanistic faith seemed to be Communism for many young people. They had heard challenging phrases such as, "The workers have nothing to lose but their chains. They have a world to win. Workers of the world, unite!" (*Manifesto of the Communist Party*, 1848). The second Five Year Plan of Russia, under Stalin, had demonstrated, however, that the classless society meant the abolition of individuals and the slavery of the masses.

No sooner had Stalin, and then Hitler, come to power than their satanic ideologies were tested out with the utmost cynicism in the Civil War in Spain. This forgotten struggle was then shaping the future of the world.

As an infantry soldier who was tested and wounded in battle, I found there was nothing in humanism to justify either fighting or surviving. It had nothing to offer but machinery, profit-and-loss, control systems, one-dimensional existence, destruction, death. A number of contemporary writers, such as Thomas Pynchon in *Gravity's Rainbow*, have seized upon this despairing faith, and classified it as *entropy*. The word "entropy" is used to refer to the breakdown of order into the disorder of chaos. May not this be an acceptable metaphor to describe humanism's destiny?

For me, the war demonstrated the hopelessness, the meaninglessness, the cynicism, the emptiness, the nothingness of humanism. As a faith it led to despair, death and the empty void.

Set against this life-negating faith, I witnessed, and then experienced, the life-giving power of the Christ-centered faith. By the faithfulness of a few of His followers, new life was given to me. I became a disciple, maybe reluctantly, because there was nowhere else I could turn for life—and the words of life—but to Jesus, the Word who became flesh.

To be realistic I had to recognize there are two faiths. The arguments I had heard in my student days, about humanism being rational and scientific, and the Christian faith being irrational, obsolete and absurd seemed so stupid to me now.

There are two faiths! One that fails, and one that triumphs. One that affirms death, and one that affirms life. One that rejects authentic human existence, and one that exalts it. One that denies God and man, and one that praises God and serves His people.

2

Two Faiths—
Humanism and Christianity

The similarities and differences of the two faiths.
At many a university gathering, I have heard these words of Alexander Pope (1688-1744) quoted from *An Essay on Man*:

Know then thyself, presume not God to scan;
The proper study of mankind is man.

They have been used as an undeniable statement, as the expression of a self-evident truth of an absolute nature. This statement has become a slogan of contemporary humanism.

The words have a reasonable ring to them. Why not study man, his habits, his actions, his environment, his history, his civilizations, his ideas, his artistic forms and his sciences? Surely we could learn a great deal from such a study. Since Pope's time, this has been done. The extent of such study could be measured by the proliferation of knowledge about the natural and social sciences. But what have we really learned?

Before we look more closely at this question, let us scan the similarities between the two faiths. Both claim to uphold the importance of human existence. Both stress the wisdom of altruism. Both espouse a moral concern. Both emphasize human liberty.

Those who take the name of Christ have much to

11

learn from the moral expressions of humanists. This is something that is often pointed out by them. The historical record cites dreadful cases of inhumane behavior on the part of Christians. In the name of Christ, people have fought with each other, violently disagreed with each other and killed each other. From the fourth century A.D. on, churchmen assigned heretics to the civil powers for execution. By the thirteenth century, the Emperor of the Holy Roman Empire was given the right to try and condemn those accused of heresy. The history of the Inquisition is well known, and it is detestable. Under John Calvin's leadership in Geneva, heretics were killed. Lest we think such horrors are things of the past, let us face the fact that in the 1950s an American evangelist coined the slogan, "Kill a Communist for Christ." And many avowed Christians upheld a similar, if less crudely expressed, conviction.

Why were so many Christians so indifferent for so long to the plight of the white slaves and then the black slaves, or to the cause of peace, or the condition of the poor, or the misery of prisoners, or the exploitation of women and children?

The examples of humanists have often been so much better than those of people in organized religions. The German theologian Hans Küng in his splendid book, *On Being a Christian*, points out that in the Imperial Constantinian Church, "pagan anti-Judaism was given a 'Christian' stamp," and that Jews were slaughtered in the first three crusades. On the other hand, humanism was instrumental in bringing about the change necessary for the acceptance of Jews as fellow human beings.

In terms of the civil rights movement, the peace movement, and the rights of laborers, so often it is those of a humanist persuasion who have been in the vanguard. They have demonstrated by their actions what Christians should have been doing in the name of Jesus.

Instead of listing humanist organizations that have made genuine contributions to the well-being of mankind, let me give a few examples from my own experience on campus.

I came to the U.S.A. and to Princeton University at the time of the Montgomery bus boycott. This began when a seamstress, Rosa Parks, entered a bus to go home after a hard day's work. There was no room in the section assigned to blacks, so she sat down in the "white section." When a white man entered, the bus driver ordered Mrs. Parks to give him her seat. She was weary, and her feet hurt, so she refused. The driver stopped the bus and called a policeman, who promptly arrested her.

The Rev. Dr. Martin Luther King, Jr., became the leader in the struggle for the freedom of his people. I admired him for this, and contributed a little toward the financial support of his movement. On two occasions he preached for me in the University Chapel. Both times his sermons were evangelical, compassionate and relevant. I was, however, severely criticized by two groups, both of which wished me to be fired. One was a group of wealthy people who wished to maintain the economic *status quo*. It was not surprising that such a group should object; what was surprising was that another group, which classified themselves as conservative Christians, should object loudly and angrily. There were, of course, Christians who stood by me. I was not surprised at that, but I was surprised when a number of humanists came to my support. They did so because of their belief in human freedom. In doing so, they not only had my gratitude, but perhaps, the respect of St. James who wrote, "Pure religion and undefiled before God and the Father is this, To visit the fatherless and widows in their affliction, and to keep himself unspotted from the world" (James 1:27).

I cite this example to remind myself that the ethical practices of humanists often exceed those of Christians. Although Christians fail continuously, Christ does not. This, I think, marks the difference between Christians and humanists.

I shall let a humanist philosopher speak for himself. In his introduction to a series of essays entitled, *Objections to Humanism*, H.J. Blackham points out that Christian morality cannot be separated from faith in Christ. This means nothing to the humanist. Blackham writes, "There is no supreme example of humanist ethics, because, on humanist assumptions, there is no *summum bonum*, no chief end of all action, no far-off crowning event to which all things exist, no teleology, no definitive human nature even." This reads like a Christian's criticism of humanism, a criticism that is in agreement with Paul's great statement: "For by him were all things created, that are in heaven, and that are in earth, visible and invisible, whether they be thrones, or dominions, or principalities, or powers: all things were created by him, and for him: And he is before all things, and by him all things consist. And he is the head of the body, the church: who is the beginning, the first-born from the dead; that in all things he might have the preeminence. For it pleased the Father that in him should all fulness dwell" (Col. 1:16-19).

For the Christian, this is a heady and inspiring summing up of his faith. For the humanist, such a faith is nonsense. The opinion of Bertrand Russell in his *Human Society in Ethics and Politics* is, "All faiths do harm. We may define 'faith' as a firm belief in something for which there is no evidence. When there is evidence no one speaks of 'faith.' "

I would, of course, answer Lord Russell by saying, "You may be quite correct, but remember, both of us are speaking from evidence. You are talking about the evidence you perceive in the sphere of discernible phenomena as you measure it by the positive sciences. I would not disagree with your position. I would, however, say it is a limited one. As a Christian, I center my faith on the person, life and works of Jesus. Because I do, I claim that through my knowledge of Him I have knowledge of God and His cosmos."

The Field of Discernment.

It is in the day-to-day experiences of existence that we make our judgments about ourselves, our neighbors, our destiny, our sense of meaning and purpose, our way of living, our moral standards, but above all, our decision for or against Christ and God.

According to the faith of the humanist we possess the freedom to create our own life style without reference to a power, or being, or person outside ourselves. The rationalists believe reason is the one facet of human existence which may be abstracted and given absolute value. Reason itself is, of course, the norm of judgment. And this, according to the humanist, is a quality that everyone possesses as a consequence of the accident of nature. Reason has replaced God; therefore, Alexander Pope could write: "Know then thyself, presume not God to scan."

Those of you who are familiar with the thought of René Descartes, particularly as it is expressed in his *Discourse on Method*, will recognize why this thought is often referred to as the hypothesis of the modern period. Descartes believed man's essential nature consisted only of thinking. Thinking, in turn, is the evidence of reason. As the title of the book suggests, Descartes was only interested in establishing a rational method of inquiry. His famous dictum, *"cogito ergo sum"* ("I think, therefore I am"), pervades the thinking of humanists.

This kind of faith I found thoroughly inadequate to deal with my condition as a human being who existed as an imperfect being, in an imperfect world, with imperfect neighbors. Whatever I was, I was a person who lived and feared and hoped and sinned and loved. My reason and my thinking were possible only because I existed in the first place. Even at my most highly exalted rationalistic moments, such as when I was writing an essay on the superiority of pure reason, I was aware that my reason was not pure, and my logic was faulty.

No matter how rational I tried to be, I was dogged by my own irrationality, my own mortality, my own feelings, my own will, my own consciousness. My logical answers were never quite the same as the logical answers of my fellow rationalists. Indeed, rationalists in Germany were postulating conclusions that were remarkably different from those of rationalists in England.

Descartes' belief is one which is ever popular on campuses. It suits the intellectual climate (i.e., the belief in pure reason, the ultimacy of the logical process and the analyses of externals by the method of the positive sciences). As a faith, it seems to exalt man while denying God. Pascal rightly criticized Descartes in *Pensées*: "In all his philosophy he would have been quite willing to dispense with God. But he had to make Him give a fillip to set the world in motion; beyond this, he has no further need of God." This is the position of the *deists*. If, however, God is only the prime mover necessary for logic, then He is less significant than reason itself. He is the necessary cause and nothing more.

Apart from my own experiences, the best criticism I know of Descartes' unexamined faith is to be found in a book by the Spanish philosopher, Miguel De Unamuno, *Tragic Sense of Life:* "The defect in Descartes' *Discourse on Method* . . . lies in his resolving to begin by leaving himself out, omitting Descartes, the real man, the man of flesh and blood, the man who does not want to die, so that he can become a mere thinker, that is, an abstraction. . . . Is pure thought possible, knowledge without feeling, without that kind of materiality which feeling lends to it?"

Along with Unamuno's penetrating criticism is the criticism of history. Instead of producing an intellectual paradise, the age of reason produced the industrial revolution, and the age of technocracy. It produced an age in which man is denigrated to the level of a digit on "the bottom line."

The logic of rational ultimacy is plainly seen in Adam Smith's economic theory articulated in his *An Inquiry into the Nature and Causes of the Wealth of Nations*; it is also advanced in John Locke's political rationalism as seen in *Second Treatise of Government*, and in Jeremy Bentham's *An Introduction to the Principals of Morals and Legislation*. The rationalistic interpretation of commerce reduced the working man to the mechanistic level of a machine churning out a product called labor, a product to be sold in the common market according to the laws of supply and demand. For Locke, whose influence on American thought has been considerable, good and evil were merely a matter of pleasure and pain. Thus, the ultimate standard of moral and political action becomes the pleasure of the majority. On this basis, people may be thought of as being free and equal. They ought not to bring pain to each other, and ought to live in such a way that they preserve the pleasure of others, providing their own pleasure is not impaired. Although Locke refers to God, it is only as though He were an absentee landlord. Because God has fashioned people with similar natures and faculties, therefore all are to be regarded as mutually independent. Thus, everyone is duty-bound to preserve his own life and protect his own interests. Is not this a long way from the position upheld by Jesus: "Sell whatsoever thou hast, and give to the poor; . . . and come, take up the cross and follow me" (Matt. 10:21)?

If you would like to understand the logical conclusion to Bentham's utilitarianism, read Aldous Huxley's *Brave New World*. It is all there in startling *bas-relief*. Many a Christian may talk glibly about "the greatest happiness of the greatest number" without realizing he is not only talking through a hole in his hat, but speaking as one who disbelieves the gospel. God does not love the majority, He loves the whole world. Our Lord did not die for the majority, but for everyone who believes in Him. And love, not pleasure, is the ultimate good. Numbers, measurement and quantity meant everything to Bentham. So much so that he could write the following nonsense: "Quantity of pleasure being equal, pushpin is as good as poetry." For the sake of pleasure, people will obey useful rules and so will rats as B.F. Skinner has demonstrated so successfully.

Bentham signals the tragedy of rationalism in his essential teaching: "The only interests, which a man is at all times sure to find adequate motives for consulting, are his own." Again, it is a long way from the cross to this avowal of selfishness. In his work *Deontology*, published posthumously, Bentham underlines the nadir of his humanism in a reference to evil as "a miscalculation of chances." In other words, a wrong bet. His disciple John S. Mill continued Bentham's humanism in the nineteenth century. In his brief treatise on *Utilitarianism* (1861), he reduces reality to: (a) The realization of pleasure and the absence of pain; (b) The validity of desire; and (c) The ultimate good of pleasure. Therefore, he sees general happiness as the good toward which all must strive. The hedonistic magazine, *Playboy*, would agree with this position.

Although we have only touched upon the dominant thinking of the eighteenth century, we can see how similar it is to present-day thought on campuses. All of this may be summed up in a phrase borrowed from Immanuel Kant, "Rational nature exists as an end in itself."

No sooner was this statement made than it was answered by its own innate irrationalism in the reactionary mood known as romanticism. This mood provided the foundation not only for horror, such as Nazism produced, but for poetry, such as that of Wordsworth. Reason and sentiment were thus polarized as indeed Pascal prophesied they would be: "The Christian religion alone is adapted to all, being composed of externals and internals" (*Pensées*). Nineteenth-century thinkers, such as Rousseau, rebounded from the ultimacy of reason and its externals to the ultimacy of the sentiments or feelings and their internals. Having devoted his life to the cultivation of his faculties of reasoning, he came to the conclusion that there was only "one faithful guide," and that was "the chain of the sentiments" that marked the progress of his existence. Most people, when they refer to Rousseau, refer to him as an optimist. His later writings, however, reveal that such optimism is shot through with a gloomy pessimism.

In the humanism of the romantics, the "thinker of ultimate truth" is replaced by the "doer of invincible feelings." Thus, the irrationality of reason is expressed by the ultimacy of instinct, primary drives and gut feelings. Lord Byron, a distant kinsman of mine, I regret to say, was the one who gave expression to this irrationality by his life style and his poetry. Man was the god of nature, and all natural forces were his to command. Verse plays, such as *Manfred*, which developed this theme, were literally worshiped by nineteenth-century readers, most of whom were aristocrats or industrialists. The optimism and wit, which delighted his followers, however, did not sustain him in his encounter with the realities of his existence. Thus, on the eve of his thirty-sixth birthday he complains,

> My days are in the yellow leaf;
> The flowers and fruits of love are gone;
> The worm, the canker, and the grief
> Are mine alone.

This stanza might well be regarded as the prelude to twentieth-century atheistic existentialism, which is the response to nineteenth-century romanticism.

Before we consider this aspect of humanism, let us not forget the nightmarish world of Nietzsche, which the death-of-god theologians of the 1960s found so fascinating. It was he who provided them with a title for their non-theology—from his book, *Thus Spake Zarathustra*. Nietzsche saw the battle between the rationalists and the romantics as a means of interpreting Greek tragedy. This conflict was expressed in the Apollonian and Dionysian qualities of human existence. His position, however, cannot be regarded as a viable synthesis: for the Dionysian—irrational and hedonistic—qualities are seen to dominate. The influence of Nietzsche upon Hitler is greater than neo-Nietzscheanists are willing to admit, despite Hitler's own affirmation of his indebtedness to the philosopher.

The jump from romanticism to atheistic existentialism is a small one. You could say that an existentialist, such as Sartre, is a romantic who has lost his confidence in the ego's claim to ultimacy. Sartre depicts the human condition without God as the prison cell of freedom into which human beings are cast to work out their essence or meaning in despair. For Sartre no absolute existed. The closest he could come to conceiving of an absolute was the absolutism of the Communist Party. His friend, Camus, still retained a touch of the romantic, and because he did so, he became less of a friend. The writings of Sartre and Camus are so popular that their position has become the mainstay of contemporary novelists and dramatists. To be authentically human is to be aware that you are in the death cell, or in a city under the threat of a deadly plague, or in a country of exile that is the forerunner of nothing. Read Sartre's *No Exit*, and Camus' *The Fall*, and you have their basic philosophy. They will provide all the exhausted clichés necessary for cocktail conversation, or a successful novel.

Pascal, by the way, had already painted this picture of existence without God in his *Pensées*. In the section dealing with the necessity for the wager of Christian faith, he tells us that we are like prisoners in chains in the death cell waiting our turn to be executed one by one. It is indeed an honest picture of godless existence. Existence with God, by faith, however is not one of despair, but one of hope.

If I were asked my opinion of the present mood on campuses, I would have to reply, in all honesty, that it is, first of all, a mood of polarization. The conservative forces stand by the affirmations of the rationalists; the liberal forces stand by those of the romantics. Before our eyes, we see a conflict between the philosophies of the eighteenth and nineteenth centuries. In the second place, we see all too tragically the resolution of this conflict in the mood of despair, or *Angst*.

For those of you who are students of literature, it is interesting to compare classical literature with the Bible. The former is the story of the human hero trying to be God, while the latter is the story of God who became man. One is the story of human despair and death. The other is the story of faith, hope, love—and life eternal.

Contemporary existentialist literature is again the story of man who can find meaning for himself only in his despair. This is the inevitable conclusion of the faith we call humanism. We shall return to this point later. Now, however, let us look at some of the qualities of secular humanism that have been, and are, regarded as intellectually superior to the Christian faith.

3

Popular Substitutes or Secular Copies of the Christian Faith

We have to recognize that the dominance of humanism makes it difficult for intellectuals to consider the claims of Christ. They have been taught that the only permissible reality is that which may be demonstrated with the aid of the sciences, particularly mathematics, which is regarded as the symbolic language of reality. This is another way of saying that the intellect may be cut off from human experience. Detached from the senses, emotions, and the will, it is, therefore, presumed to assume a purely objective view of the external world of objects, including human beings. The center of intellectual attention is, therefore, the material world, including such invisible parts of it as molecules, atoms, electrons, neutrons, protons, and energy.

Materialism, thus, is believed to be the only tenable position for intellectuals. A professor once said to me, "Your faith seems to deal with most of the facts of human experience. I only wish it were academically acceptable." At a scientific conference some years ago, a biologist, who was giving a paper, remarked, "Evolution has been accepted by scientists, not because it has been observed to occur or proved by logical, coherent evidence to be true, but because the only alternative is clearly unacceptable." Another scientist declared, "There is clearly no place in a modern university for subjects which do not conform to scientific methods. The time has come to be ruthlessly honest and to eradicate from the curricula such subjects that fall within this classification."

These three statements are indicative of the humanistic bias of our times. In writing this, I know there are exceptions; the point is, of course, that they are *exceptions*. The method for knowing the material universe is that of positivism. Because this method cannot be applied effectively to our thinking about God and our relationship with Him, it is concluded prematurely that He and ourselves cannot be known.

The best model for this style of thinking was produced by the French philosopher Auguste Comte (1798-1857). For him, as a humanist, humanity as a whole, and as a concept, is the supreme being. The evidence of this is that it is humanity alone which discovers the ultimate (i.e., the scientific knowledge of the universe). According to this philosophy, the three stages in the development of this knowledge are:

a. *Religious knowledge:* In the days of primitive science, humanity sought to come to terms with its difficult and threatening environment by religious means. The universe was seen to be populated with mysterious and menacing forces. In order to understand, and to decrease the threats of this world to its existence, humanity ascribed human, and semi-human, characteristics to those invisible forces. Thus, good and evil spirits, demons and gods were created out of the human imagination.

b. *Philosophical knowledge:* By thinking about its sensory and imagined experiences, humanity created concepts, which in turn, reinforced the rational processes of the brain. By means of these concepts, the external universe became more manageable, and less frightening. In this way, the world as such became acceptable, and because it was acceptable, it could be known.

c. *Scientific knowledge:* Only when the positive sciences emerged, however, could the universe be known in its fullness and actuality. With the advance of science, humanity, thus, was seen as beginning to achieve its god-like potential. The scientific method displayed the immensity of the material world in terms of the metagalaxies, which seem to reach out to almost infinite space, and in terms of geological time. This material world is everything, therefore, and man is nothing.

In this light the dating of creation and natural events by biblical scholars was seen to be absurd. From 1701 until early in this century, the authorized Bibles had marginal dates beginning with creation at 4004 B.C. James Usher (1581-1656), archbishop of Armagh in Ireland, is credited with providing these dates from his *Annales Veteris et Novi Testamenti.*

Reality, as I have indicated, was reduced to physical substance. By the late nineteenth century, T.H. Huxley could say to the British Association, "The thoughts to which I am now giving utterance and your thoughts regarding them are expressions of the molecular changes in the matter of life," and apparently no one thought his statement was strange. And few would think it strange today. The soul or mind is associated with the brain, particularly, the upper stem. It is presumed that to exist at all it must be capable of physical detection. Over seventy years ago, a professor, John B. Watson of Johns Hopkins University, indicated that consciousness as such does not exist. This has been the theme of those psychologists who are lumped together under the heading of *behaviorists*. Professor Watson argued for a scientific psychology free from the fuzziness of introspection. The data essential for this investigation comes from the collection and analyses of overt responses and the stimuli that initiates them. For the behaviorist, therefore, psychology is a methodology for interpreting behavior.

B.F. Skinner is well known for his two books, *Walden II* and *Beyond Freedom and Dignity*. By his studies of rats and pigeons, he has analyzed ways whereby operant behavior may be modified through the application of negative or positive reinforcement. This is just another way of talking about punishments and rewards. *Walden II* is a novel—not a very good one—dealing with the creation of a Utopian situation through operant conditioning. The individual, as such, has no identity save that which is produced in him by his controlled environment. The controller of *Walden II* says at one point, "Give me the specifications, and I'll give you the man!" This sums up prevailing psychologies of education, which are both taught and practiced on contemporary campuses. The individual is thus treated as a material object, and Christ is ignored.

By rejecting a view of the universe as an act of creation, fulfilled by Christ's redemptive action, reality is reduced to materialistic manifestations. The absurdity of this faith is, of course, that although human beings are nothing more than gangling systems of responses, they are, nevertheless, capable of working out their own salvation, because the enlightened intellectuals—and what enlightened them?—possess the knowledge to change and determine natural laws.

This describes the horns of the dilemma on which

humanists find themselves hanging. On the one horn, humanity, or the essence of humanity, is god; on the other, this god is no more than matter, which is to say that there is neither God nor man.

Materialism as the rationalization of humanism was inadequate to explain the emerging data made possible by the sciences. The view that fundamental matter was an interrelated system of irreducible hard parts, similar to shotgun pellets or ball bearings, was made impossible by the awareness that matter was more than what it seemed. That is, ultimate matter was not those knobby little pellets, but atoms. These atoms were thought of as hypothetical particles, incapable of division, until it was conceived that even the atom could be split.

Materialism was thus replaced by "emergent evolution," "creative evolution," "the unfinished universe," "evolutionary humanism," "developing reality," and so on. These are terms illustrating attempts to grapple with the dynamic nature of matter. You have probably heard of Henri Bergson's *élan vital?* This life force is both the inner reality of ourselves, and the motivating power that drives the universe forward and upward. George Bernard Shaw introduced this concept to popular thought through some of his plays which dealt with the life force in man as "vitality with a direction." Samuel Alexander and A.N. Whitehead are, perhaps, two of the best known philosophers in this movement. Both of them, I think, have had considerable influence upon modern religious theories which compete with the cosmology of the Bible. Progress, development, and linear evolution now become everyday terms to uphold the belief of humanists that reality is continuously emerging and developing.

Alexander believed that reality is experienced at

the meeting point of space and time. We exist as "point-events," or as self-conscious entities on the line of the universe's emergence. Thus the human race evolves from lower to higher values. This evolutionary drive produces its own purpose, or plan, as it expresses itself in space-time. As this purpose is being worked out it has no end. It is endless, moving onward toward higher and yet higher points of moral existence.

As God is no longer Creator, Sustainer, Governor and Lord, how is He expected to fit into this system? The answer Alexander gives is a very naive one: God is simply the next point of emergence, "the next higher empirical quality." Such a faith, I think, demands a greater piety than most of us can contemplate.

Alfred North Whitehead (1861-1947) is the most revered prophet of this belief through his *magnum opus, Process and Reality.* He affirms that process is reality. I take it, therefore, that when we think of God's infinity we are to think in terms of the process "acquiring realization." This means that, "God is not to be treated as an exception to all metaphysical principles, invoked to save their collapse. He is their chief exemplification. Viewed as primordial he is the unlimited conceptual realization of the absolute wealth of potentiality" (*Process and Reality*).

Process as the ultimate reality is a belief that is upheld in many departments of religion, and suits the various expressions of evolutionary humanism.

The movement from a rigid materialism to the belief in a fluid, dynamic and changing universe provided the metaphysical structure for the optimism of the nineteenth century. Humanism was reinforced by Charles Darwin's theory of evolution as it was expressed in his *Origin of Species.* This theory, added to the process view of reality, produced the theory of inevitable progress. The theme song of this belief was probably written by Dr. Coué: "Every day, in every way, we are getting better and better." The belief in inevitable progress dominated the intellectual atmosphere of the nineteenth century. And, after two world wars, Korea, and Vietnam, it still prevails despite the evidence to the contrary.

According to Darwin, the dynamic of the evolutionary progress is "natural selection," or as he modified it later, "natural preservation." By the processes of nature, organisms which are inadequate are eliminated. The fittest survive, hence the phrase, "survival of the fittest"—one borrowed from Spencer. In this regard it is interesting to observe that B.F. Skinner has indicated that the fitness or worth of a nation is determined by its ability to survive. Had Nazi Germany been victorious, it would have been regarded as a good nation according to B.F. Skinner's definition, borrowed from Darwin.

Although Darwin's works deal with structures, environment, behavior and development, they were quickly absorbed into the prevailing mood of optimism with its enthusiastic proclamation of progress in every area of human existence. Society represented the peak of the evolutionary ascent, and nothing lay beyond it but more and more, and better, peaks. Evolution provided a neat formula for the theory of man. Out of the primordial soup emerged something that moved up the evolutionary escalator, through primates, until the human beings who inhabit New York, London, Paris, Berlin, Moscow, Peking and Tokyo came into being.

It has to be admitted that some of the attempts to challenge this faith have not been laudable. Thomas Huxley, the defender of Darwinism, and nicknamed

"Darwin's Bulldog," engaged in a debate with Bishop Wilberforce, a defender of special creation. At the end of the debate Bishop Wilberforce asked Huxley if he were descended from a monkey on his grandfather's side or his grandmother's side.

In his reply Huxley wiped the floor with his opponent by saying, "If there were an ancestor whom I should feel shame in recalling, it would be a man . . . who, not content with an equivocal success in his own sphere of activity, plunges into scientific questions with which he has no real acquaintance, only to obscure them by an aimless rhetoric, and distract the attention of his heavens from the real point at issue by eloquent digressions, and skilled appeals to religious prejudice."

Huxley's point is valid: before you jump at untested conclusions be sure you have your facts straight!

A crude criticism wins no converts. Recently I read a poorly prepared challenge to evolution. The writer made the following points:

a. "The doctrine of evolution displaces God, who is no longer needed as Creator." Therefore, all who use evolution as a model are atheists!

b. "The doctrine of evolution is the devil's lie." Therefore, every aspect of this doctrine is a lie.

c. "Would you want to descend from the monkey?" This question ignores the position of several theories of evolution.

A Christian view of evolution.

The points made against evolution by the author I've just quoted fail to discriminate between believers who use the doctrine of evolution as a model of creation still initiated and governed by God, and unbelievers who use the teaching for the purposes of their own atheistic faith.

James McCosh, a devout evangelical minister and philosopher, assumed a Christian view of evolution in his book, *The Religious Aspects of Evolution* (1890).

You may have heard of Henry Drummond's book, *The Greatest Thing in the World.* He was an evangelist, and a close friend of Dwight L. Moody. He was also a scientist who taught at New College, Edinburgh. His Christian interpretation of evolution is highly readable. It is published under the title, *The Ascent of Man* (1894).

In the introduction, Drummond points out that "evolution was given to the modern world out of focus." His thesis is that evolution is to be seen as "the story of creation." It is a history of the steps by which the world has come into being. As such it is to be regarded as no more than a working principle or model. The error made by most modern interpreters is that of reducing evolution to the struggle for life. This improper analysis has missed another equally prominent part of the evolutionary story, namely, the struggle for the life of others.

By emphasizing the first part, life is reduced to a selfish, hedonistic and utilitarian existence. The other view, however, deals with the development of "other-ism," which is characterized by sympathy, tenderness, unselfishness: the "mother principle."

Drummond shows that the moral order is a continuous line from the beginning. Immorality, selfishness and the sins of the Fall are the deviation from the norm. This shows that a moral order in the biological realm is the hallmark of the Creator. That which begins in the act of creation is completed, therefore, by the act of redemption. It is on this basis that he, as a scientist, criticizes other scientists for using the evolutionary theory to support their agnosticism. By doing so they limit the facts to the struggle for life, and its selfish consequences. By isolating this aspect of survival, they have missed the reality of the struggle for the life of others. Creation would regress to stagnation and death without it. This is the only end of selfishness: "Had there been no altruism—altruism in the definite sense of unselfishness, sympathy, and self-sacrifice for others, the whole higher world of life had perished as soon as it was created. For hours, or days, or weeks in the early infancy of all higher animals, maternal care and sympathy are a condition of existence. Altruism had to enter the world, and any species which neglected it was extinguished in a generation" (*The Ascent of Man*).

Somewhat along the same lines, Albert Schweitzer worked out his doctrine of *Reverence for Life*. The incident that triggered his thinking was a very simple one. It was that of seeing one hippopotamus helping another at a moment of difficulty in a river. In its way, the hippopotamus was concerned with the other. To Schweitzer, this was an example of the stronger helping the weaker, and a denial of the selfishness principle of the survival of the fittest.

Perhaps we may conclude that an atheist who uses his secular faith to deny God must inevitably end up by denying creation. The Christian, on the other hand, by affirming God as the Creator, is able to see God's purpose being worked out within creation itself, and in accord with Christ's atoning and reconciling sacrifice, whereby the world is reconciled to its Creator.

The Biblical View

The Bible does not present us with a static picture of creation. It is a dynamic image. Indeed, it is bound to be powerful because it is according to God's active

Word. There is nothing accidental about it. It is by divine intent. The sense of God willing it to be so is very clear. The first sentence of Genesis seems to be a great proclamation announcing the revelation that the whole universe, or cosmos, is the evidence of the living God's activity. The second sentence may well give us the first stage by which creation came into being. The earth was, "without form, and void," a veritable wasteland, or chaos, or primordial disorder, waiting for the divine Word to direct its future.

After the statement of revelation and the description of the earth's earliest condition, we are given the sequence of orderly creation which occurs in six stages or days.

1. *The first stage is the creation of light.* This light is the source, or means, of order and life. Without such order there can be no life. Having delighted in the creation of light, God then "separated the light from the darkness." What is this but a description of the sun and the moon and the planets and the stars and the galaxies and the metagalaxies set in motion against the darkness of space? Thus, in our daily experience, we have the awareness of this order which is as clear as night and day. This awareness of order had a great deal to do with the development of astronomy, and the sciences in general. These words of Immanuel Kant (1724-1804) come to mind in this respect:

> Two things fill the mind with ever-increasing wonder and awe the more often and the more intensely the mind of thought is drawn to them: the starry heavens above me and the moral law within me (*Critique of Practical Reason*)

2. *The second stage was the creation of the "firmament."* The picture we are given is that of solid substances

emerging in the midst of the waters as though what is now the planet earth was nothing but a churning mass of water. Thus the creation of both the waters and the dry land indicates the logical step from light to inorganic forms of creation, particularly as they relate to the earth.

3. *In the third stage we see the gathering of the waters under the heavens in an orderly fashion followed by the appearance of dry land which is named earth.* The setting is now ready, therefore, for the creation of organic substances such as forms of grass, lichens, mosses, and so on, which prepare the necessary soil for grain-yielding grasses and fruit-bearing trees. In this way the cycle of organic reproduction is established and the fruitfulness of earth assured.

4. *The fourth stage establishes the means of this fruitfulness and is a logical continuation of the second day.* The sun rises, its creative light makes growth possible, and it is *day.* With the setting of the sun comes night and rest. By this order the time for days, seasons and years is set. Time as we know it begins. Along with the sun and moon is the lesser light of the stars. We are to see the sun, moon and metagalaxies as serving God by taking their place in time. It was this understanding that saved the Israelites from the cults which ascribed divinity to the sun and the stars.

5. *In the fifth stage the waters are to be productive like the earth.* The order is interesting. First there are "swarming things." This suggests a great richness or fertility. Second, the birds fly. Third, come the great maritime mammals, every kind of living creature which swam in the water. Then every kind of winged bird. Fish and birds are now part of the reproductive cycle.

6. *The final stage of the sixth day is the creation of all*

cattle, all reptiles, small quadrupeds, insects, and wild animals.

The peak of creation is reached with the creation of man. The importance of this is emphasized in the deliberate decision of God: "Let us make man in our image, after our likeness: and let them have dominion over the fish of the sea, and over the fowl of the air, and over the cattle, and over all the earth, and over every creeping thing that creepeth upon the earth" (Gen. 1:26). It should be noted that "dominion" does not mean "exploit" as some contemporary ecologists have stated. It means "to care for and to be responsible for, under the sovereignty of God."

The reference to the first human being as created in God's image is so important I shall discuss it under a separate section dealing with the Christian view of man.

Those are the six stages of creation. The Jesuit paleontologist, Pierre Teilhard de Chardin (1881-1955), seems to have used a similar series of stages in his, *The Phenomenon of Man.* He outlines the order: "Before life came" (i.e., the stage of the inorganic); "Life" (the organic stage); "Thought" or consciousness; "Survival" (leading to the completion and salvation of all things through Christ who is the *Alpha* and *Omega*).

More important than these stages, however, are the two great affirmations of the Bible: "In the beginning God created the heaven and the earth," and "In the beginning was the Word, and the Word was with God, and the Word was God." These are the two poles of Christian cosmology.

1. The world is God's by creation. It was created out of nothing. By this act, space and time originate. To say, "In the beginning," is to say that creation passes from

non-being into being. Thus, direction, purpose and destiny are implicit in the act of creation.

Because the world exists, we do not need to prove its existence. This may look like a silly statement, but it is not. There are those who have to prove the existence of creation because the only reality they may affirm is that of their own reason, or the *panthos* (i.e., the totality of all things). Having accepted the reality of creation and time because they are there, we have a foundation on which to build a world view that makes scientific methods and understanding possible. By itself there is no necessity for the world's existence. The world did not have to exist until God spoke. Thus, the cause, purpose, destiny and governance of creation and creatures are beyond, or outside, themselves. This is the point St. Paul makes in Romans 4:17, "God, who quickeneth the dead, and calleth those things which be not as though they were." Today's English Version puts it this way, "The God who brings the dead to life and whose command brings into being what did not exist."

We may say that the real existence of ourselves and the universe is given by God. Because it is, it is other than God in the way that a piece of sculpture is other than the sculptor, yet is dependent upon the sculptor for its existence. In our case, as human beings, we may say that creation assures our freedom: for by creating us, God has set us free in an existence that is separate from His own. Thus, the Fall takes place in creation, in the freedom that creation ensures.

The revelation of creation, as we have discussed earlier, is contrary to the belief of popular humanism. Because it is, freedom, purpose, destiny, sin and goodness are beyond the range of the humanist's conception; and because they are, there is nothing left but "one dimensional" or "wasteland" existence, if this truth is ignored.

Along with humanism, classical, Hellenistic, and Oriental thought suffer the same fate. Only those who have accepted the revelation of the Bible may say, "The heavens declare the glory of God" (Ps. 19:1), or "What is man that thou art mindful of him?" (Ps. 8:4). Those who are brought up in the Christian faith often fail to realize how important the emphasis upon creation is. The creation is capable of redemption, and therefore, it is hopeful. Just to say, "In the beginning God created," is to take the first step toward the gospel.

I have often read through the Acts of the Apostles and passed over the incident in Lystra when Paul and Barnabas were worshiped as gods without thinking about the reasons for such enthusiasm. The principal reason is found in these words of St. Paul: "The good news we bring tells you to turn from these follies to the living God, who made heaven and earth and sea and everything in them. In past ages he allowed all nations to go their own way; and yet he has not left you without some clue to his nature, in the kindness he shows: he sends you rain from heaven and crops in their seasons, and gives you food and good cheer in plenty" (Acts 14:15-17, NEB).

On reading this, you might think, "What is so great about so simple a fact? It is only a reference to creation and the covenant of creation made with Noah. Everyone knows that." Everyone may, today, in the churches of the U.S.A., but the Lycaonians did not, and neither do many people in this twentieth century.

In his autobiography, *Memories, Dreams, Reflections,* Carl Jung tells us of a visit he made to Africa in 1926. While in Kenya he conversed with the people about their religious beliefs. He learned they believed in two gods. The good god was the sun at the moment of rising, and only then. For that brief moment *manu* reigned. At night the evil spirit *ayik* ruled the earth. Under his reign, the earth was filled with monsters, vicious animals and destructive spirits. During the night, the people lived in dread. It is in the despair and darkness of such dread that the biblical faith shines, proclaiming that this is God's world, and that His beloved Son died for it: "I believe in God the Father Almighty, Maker of heaven and earth: And in Jesus Christ his only Son our Lord" (Apostles' Creed).

2. The old covenant—or Old Testament—however, does not tell the whole story. What begins with the living God's creative act is completed by His redemptive, or re-creative act: "The Word become flesh." This act we know as the Incarnation began in Mary, in the cave, in Bethlehem, and was completed on the cross at Golgotha, the wasteland, or no man's land outside the walls of Jerusalem. That cross marks the end of the old creation, the old covenant, and the old man or Adam; and the initiation of the new creation and age, the new covenant and hope, the new or second Adam and the new community of faith, the Body of Christ. At the seventeenth verse of the fifth chapter of Matthew's Gospel, Jesus says, "Think not that I have come to abolish the law and the prophets; I have come not to abolish them but to fulfil them" (RSV).

This passage may refer to the criticisms leveled at Jesus by scribes and Pharisees, namely, that He violated the righteousness of the Law or Torah by healing on the Sabbath contrary to the Law, and by keeping company with tax collectors and sinners, that is, those who were outside the Law's standard of righteousness. The Greek word for "fulfill" or "complete" refers to the kind of completion that occurs when a void is filled.

Although Jesus abolishes the Old Covenant, and the old Israel, He does so by filling their void of inadequacy. Thus, as He fulfills Scripture and prophecies, so does he fulfill all righteousness (Matt. 3:15), and He demands that His people of the New Covenant fulfill, or exceed, the righteousness of the scribes and Pharisees (Matt. 5:20).

By the completion of creation, our Lord has indeed made all things new (Rev. 21:5). We live in the new age in the power of our Lord's resurrection. St. Paul tells us that the first man, or Adam, was a living soul, but the last Adam is the Lord from heaven (1 Cor. 15:45). A very clear explanation of this completion is to be found in the fifth chapter of Romans, where St. Paul tells us that the consequence of justification by faith is that we are put right with God. Because we are, we have peace and we are brought into the experience and dimension of grace in which we live. In the second century, Irenaeus of Lyons said, "The Son of God became the Son of man, that man also might become the son of God." In saying this, Irenaeus was revealing biblical understanding of the intent, purpose and achievement of redemption.

It is important to realize that the Greek, and particularly, the Platonic influence, has emphasized the Fall as that from a state of innocence or perfection. As a consequence of this emphasis the position of Irenaeus has been overlooked. His, I think, is a more biblical one. Accordingly, we are to understand that Adam is part of creation although he is a "living soul." He was incomplete in the sense that he did not, or would not, trust and obey God wholeheartedly. His disobedience is the Fall. In distinguishing between the "image" and "likeness" of God, Irenaeus tried to show that the "likeness" referred to the quality of personal

39

existence which is a reflection of the divine life. Man, as the "image of God" is, therefore, only the first stage in the creative plan. It is in Jesus that we see the completion of God's creative purpose and intent. The eighth chapter of the Epistle to the Romans illustrates this truth.

1. Christ has set us free from "the law of sin and death" (8:2).
2. God has done for us what the law could not do. He condemned sin and human imperfection by sending His own Son in the flesh (8:3).
3. The fulfilled life which Christ offers is in "the spirit of Christ" (8:9).
4. By our Lord's resurrection, His followers have been given new life while in their mortal bodies (8:11).
5. All those "who are led by the Spirit of God are sons of God" (8:14).
6. The hope of creation is that it will be liberated from its bondage to enjoy, "the glorious liberty of the children of God" (8:21).
7. By faith we may discern the good end toward which creation moves, for we have seen the nature of this good end in Jesus (8:28).
8. By the fulfillment of creation, in, and through Jesus, God has established the new humanity of the second Adam. As "the first-born among many brethren" (8:29), He is the elder brother of the new people of God. The first, that is, within the new creation.

It is on the basis of this completed creation that we may think of ourselves as children of God, members of Christ's body, the Church, and heirs of eternity. There is nothing small about the redeeming work of Jesus. Salvation is not, therefore, a matter of people pulling themselves up to heaven by their own shoelaces, or waiting until the evolutionary escalator dumps us in the evolutionary Utopia. Salvation is a matter of trusting in Jesus as Lord, and living in the power of the Holy Spirit within the new community of faith, hope and love.

Usually we think of change taking place through the use of physical force. This has been the theme of revolutionaries over the past 300 years. Change, however, in biblical terms, comes by the transforming power of the Spirit. When Christ was crucified and raised from the dead, Caesar was in power, and remained in power. Indeed, the Roman Empire was reaching its peak. Tyranny, persecution, slavery and sins of every kind continued. Nearly 2,000 years later, tyrants are still in power and sins flourish. What is the Christian answer to this fact?

I can think of two possible answers: (a) In our natural thinking we tend to give priority to externals. Reality is conceived in spatial, temporal and physical terms and symbols. Our heroes, for example, are symbols of power—George Washington, Abraham Lincoln, Dwight D. Eisenhower, the president of IBM, ITT, the occupant of the White House, and so on. Good as they may be as persons, their goodness, however, is only measured by their military victories, the GNP, the number of votes, their control of people, the bottom line of the budget, the amount of property, and so on.

Jesus was concerned with none of these. He was the God/man who died on the cross as a rebel for the world's salvation. He had no kingdom of this world, no armies, no court of pomp and circumstance, no money. According to the prevailing faith of secular Americans in success He was a failure. In His teaching He advises us not to store up treasure on earth, but treasure in heaven. We are to love our enemies, and pray for our persecutors. We are not to be anxious about tomorrow. Read the Sermon on the Mount! What does it emphasize? This teaching of Jesus displays the reality of the inner or spiritual life! It is what comes out of us, rather than what goes in, that counts. It is not the external features, but the internal qualities, that matter. And what is this but the spiritual life in the power of the Holy Spirit? St. Paul has given us the fruits, or works, of the Spirit: "love, joy, peace, patience, kindness, goodness, faithfulness, gentleness, and self-control; against such there is no law" (Gal. 5:22, 23 RSV).

When we speak about dying to the world to live in Christ, we are recognizing that we are allowing the Holy Spirit to transform us from the image of the old Adam and his sins to the image of the second Adam and His holiness. This transformation is individual, because it is taking place within each of us as persons. It is also communal, because it is taking place, generation by generation within the community of faith, the fellowship of the Holy Spirit. As Reinhold Niebuhr has pointed out, the Church is where the kingdom of God impinges upon this world. To be a Christian is to be a member of Christ's community, and to share in His redeeming work day by day. Our citizenship is in heaven. This leads me to my second point.

b. *Salvation is now.* Our well-being does not exist in some Utopian situation in the future. It exists now. We are being made well, being transformed into Christ's likeness—*now.* When Martha told Jesus she believed in the Resurrection in the future, at the time of the event known to the Jews as the Last Day, Jesus replied by using his divine title, "I AM," and by saying, "I am the resurrection, and the life: he that believeth in me, though he were dead, yet shall he live: and whosoever liveth and believeth in me shall never die" (John 11:25, 26).

This emphasis upon salvation and life now is unique to the Christian faith. Every individual in his own place and time is precious in God's sight, and is within God's purpose. We know what this purpose is: for we see it fulfilled in Jesus. He is our origin, and our destiny. Our origin, and our destiny are in Him who is the *Alpha* and the *Omega*. Through faith in Him, we share in His eternal life although we are still in our mortal bodies.

Galatians 2:20 helps us to understand what it means to be a Christian here and now. "I am crucified with Christ: nevertheless I live; yet not I, but Christ liveth in me: and the life which I now live in the flesh I live by the faith of the Son of God, who loved me, and gave himself for me." As I understand this great passage, to be crucified with Christ is to be set free from the control of sin, and liberated for our new life in Christ. The consequence of this conversion is the new life of forgiveness and joy in our relationship with Christ and his brothers and sisters. The key to our salvation now is in these words: "Yet not I, but Christ liveth in me." Our salvation and new life are not of, and by, ourselves. We are not yet fully grown. We still know only in part. We have not yet come into our full spiritual maturity. We are on the way. Our present life in the body is lived by faith in the Son of God. He gives us the power to live, to be renewed, and to grow into His likeness.

Our new life is never finished. We may never sit still and presume we have arrived, that we have made it. Such a position is a denial of eternal life. For one thing, our God is the living God. You may recall that when

King David wanted to build a great temple to hold His presence, God revealed to Nathan the prophet that he was not a God who dwelt in temples, but one who goes from one campsite to the next. And for another, our individual lives are not completed in any temporal/secular situation, but in the eternal. It is in this understanding that the writer of the Letter to the Hebrews compares the Christian's life to a pilgrimage, "For here we have no continuing city, but we seek one to come" (Heb. 13:14).

To sum up the reality of our life in Christ here and now, I would describe it as a route march in grace on the way to the fullness of glory.

True and false optimism.

The Christian position is optimistic. We have passed from death to life; from despair to hope; from misery to glory. This optimism has been copied by humanism. The confluence of rationalism, romanticism and evolutionary materialism produced a belief in inevitable progress. This belief presumed that the material world had a built-in purpose and direction. It cannot help but progress from point A to point B in history. Point A is, of course, the inadequate beginning; and point B is the desired, or imagined, good in the future.

It seems simplistic. Do not laugh at it too readily. It is the faith in which all of us in the United States have been reared. We have been nurtured to believe in success and in good old Yankee know-how. From rags to riches, log cabin to White House, village cottage to city penthouse! The good man in many congregations is the one who is president of the bank and has made a million, rather than a poor man who has sold all for Christ. In the academic sphere it has been presumed that once you attain a Ph.D. you do not need Christian faith any longer; you know better. Certain magazines and advertisements remind us that we are on the way to the better life through better technology. Indeed, the best thing we can do is to put our lives into the hands of a certain insurance company which will ensure the better life. In the sixties, Harold Wilson, prime minister of Great Britain, proclaimed we were at the beginning of a great era of prosperity made possible by technology. President Johnson promised us the Great Society along with "guns and butter." Thus, in every way, we were getting better and better.

Rationalism presumes that by the aid of pure reason—whatever that may be—the purely rational, rationalized, society will come into being in which everyone will live rationally and happily evermore.

Romanticism presumes we have the power within us to rule as gods, controlling the elemental forces of the cosmos. These forces are our servants and they are at our mercy; because they are, we may create the perfect society. For many, the belief of romanticism is summed up in these well-known verses of William E. Henley (1849-1903).

Out of the night that covers me,
Black as the Pit from pole to pole,
I thank whatever gods may be
For my unconquerable soul.

In the fell clutch of circumstance,
I have not evinced nor cried aloud:
Under the bludgeonings of chance
My head is bloody, but unbowed.

It matters not how straight the gate,
How charged with punishments the scroll,
I am the master of my fate;
I am the captain of my soul.

If such is the case, then there is not anything I cannot do. I can create the heaven that others in the past have failed to do. There is an optimism here that may be more characteristic of early youth than of age and experience.

Psychologisms are another form of this faith. The chief prophet of this approach was Sigmund Freud. He believed, and shared his belief, that abnormal, antisocial behavior may be understood as an interplay of inward forces known as the ego, superego and id. Religion is displaced by psychology. Freud referred to the mythology of ancient Greece as a norm, particularly the norm of Oedipus. "We are reminded that the hero of the Oedipus legend too felt guilty for his actions and punished himself, although the compulsion of the oracle should have made him innocent in our judgment and in his own. The super-ego is in fact the heir to the Oedipus complex and only arises after that complex has been disposed of" *(An Outline of Psychoanalysis).*

Once disposed of, our aggressive and destructive drives will disappear. I need not refer further to Freud's belief, for our literature and pop psychology are steeped in it. It has to be admitted that his followers have been more simplistic and optimistic than he was. They have carried to extremes his views that Christianity must be false because it is not scientific, and that it is in itself a neurosis out of which people grow when they become better educated. Once we perceive that God the Father is nothing more than the projection of our own experience of parental authority, we and society are thus on the way to better health and better everything. The happy ending for mankind will occur when we are all psychoanalyzed. As someone, rather unkindly, has said, "Neurotics build castles in the air; psychotics inhabit them, and pay the rent to their psychiatrists." We may learn from Freud, but we need not deify him. Anyone may need the help of a psychiatrist; but if he does, it is better, as C.S. Lewis indicates, to choose a Christian one. The point we have to remember is that "psychologisms" do not, and cannot, take the place of God's reality and the reality of the cosmos created by Him.

Marxism is a clear example of the optimism that is centered upon the belief in the inevitability of progression toward the desirable good end. Marx, as a left-wing Hegelian, and member of the young doctor's group, applied Hegel's theory of a dynamic universe to the social dimension of existence. The formula of Hegel's dialectic is a familiar one:

THESIS ——————————— ANTITHESIS

SYNTHESIS

Thus, the Marxist formula for dialectical materialism is:

BOURGEOIS ————— PROLETARIAT
(Owners of industry)   (The working class)

CLASSLESS SOCIETY

Marx looked toward the future happiness of all mankind as a consequence of this social dynamic. He and his followers were the enlightened ones who were aware of this historical stream flowing towards its inevitable destination or synthesis. By sharing this awareness, Marxists believe they are hastening on the coming of the classless society. For them, inevitable progress is associated with inevitable revolution.

Whereas *psychologisms* reduce individuals to puppets controlled by the forces of the subconscious, *Marxism* reduces individuals to the collective society of the future. As this society does not, as yet, exist, this means that individual existence in the present is meaningless. Man, as man, does not exist as a particular person. For Marxism, *man* is the classless society and the classless society is man. Thus, there is only the universal and ideal expression of man. Lenin was the great prophet of Marxism. He declared it was the only truth, and as such it had done away with religious superstition and bourgeois oppression.

We may see Marxism as the secularization of the gospel, and about this I shall say more at the end of this chapter. Marx was a Christian in his youth. His family turned to Christ, and he with them. In his Abitur essays, he shows his sense of commitment. One of them is a homily on St. John 15:1-14 written to reveal "the reason, essence, necessity and effect of the union of believers with Christ." Between 1835 and 1841, Marx's position changed to one of radical atheism. W. Kransnow attributes this change to "his infatuation with the romantic poetry." Whatever the cause of his change, it was marked by his rejection of Christianity as immoral and by his attempts to reduce the kingdom of God to the classless society.

One might suspect that Marx's new hatred of Christ is an indication of his desire to be the Messiah of the kingdom of the secular: a kingdom he expected to be populated with a new humanity. Although this new humanity is yet to be, it is presumed to have its origin and end in the purely material. Surely this is only one way of saying that individuals are nothing more than appearances within the reality of matter who do not, as yet, exist. The tragedy of the collective society, envisioned by Marx, is vividly portrayed by Martin Buber in these words from his *Between Man and Man:* "Dialogue and monologue are silenced. Bundled together men march without *Thou* and without *I*, those of the left who want to abolish memory, and those of the right who want to regulate it; hostile and separated hosts, they march into the common abyss."

Evolutionary Humanism is possibly the most optimistic expression of the belief in inevitable progress, particularly as it is articulated by Julian Huxley, grandson of Thomas Huxley, in his book, *Religion Without Revelation.* This was first published in 1929, and republished as a new and revised edition in 1957. He predicts that his form of "revelation-less" religion will bridge the gap between science and what old-fashioned religion once tried to affirm. He confesses he experienced a great sense of "spiritual relief" when he rejected the hypothesis of God as being supernatural. He admits it is necessary to believe something, and, although this is true, he suggests it is also essential not to believe without evidence, which, of course, means scientific evidence of observable phenomena.

I would not deny the importance of the scientific method. For by it we are able to understand something, if not everything, of the physical universe in which we exist. I do not believe, however, that the positive sciences are the means by which we are brought face to face with ultimate reality, the living God. Only faith as the response to the outreach of grace may do this. The study of the physical universe will help us to understand it, and even help us to understand it as more than it appears to be. I cannot, however, see why God has to limit himself to the competence of the scientific method, and still be God. Huxley, on the other hand, thinks of the faith we are classifying under the general description of *humanism*.

In achieving his goal, Huxley rejects God and the possibility of God. In doing so he supports the thesis I am upholding in this book; for while he maintains the necessity of faith, he cannot accept that it has a source beyond the natural world. Thus, he writes, "A personal God, to be Jehovah, or Allah, or Apollo, or Amen-Ra, or without name but simply God, I *know* nothing of. . . . Therefore I disbelieve in a personal God in any sense in which that phrase is ordinarily used." He then describes religion as ". . . a way of life. It is a way of life which follows necessarily from a man's holding certain things in reverence, from his feeling and believing them to be sacred" *(Religion Without Revelation).*

I know of Hindus who hold cows, machinery, and even killing to be sacred, as in the case of the Thugs. According to the *Playboy* ethic, lust is given an almost sacred quality. Thus, I do not find Huxley's interpretation of religion to be particularly helpful.

Having rejected the God who makes the Christian religion possible, he then goes on to reject what Christians believe to be the uniqueness of individual human beings. "All that the individual is provided with in infancy are certain broad innate tendencies or instincts, certain capacities of sensation and perception, and certain capacities of remembering, learning, and profiting by experience. There are no such things as innate ideas: the mind is a blank slate, not yet written upon." One wonders who is going to do the writing, and how a blank slate, or *tabula rasa*, profits by experience? All Huxley can tell us is that it happens according to the evolutionary drive. What we regard as spiritual forces are "a part of nature just as much as the material forces." Thus, "gods are products of the human mind just as much as scientific 'laws of nature.'"

His solution to the problem of human existence and destiny is to recognize evolutionary biology as the new instrument for realizing old-fashioned religious needs. His belief is centered in these words, "The picture of the universe provided by modern science is of a single process of self-transformation, during which new possibilities can be realized. There has been a creation of new actualities during cosmic time; it has been progressive, and it has been a self-creation."

We may regard this as an optimistic summing up of the faith we call humanism.

By this time, I hope I have illustrated some of the ways in which this faith has influenced popular opinion and thought patterns. We most certainly find it dominating the attitudes on campuses, but not only there; it is also greatly influential in politics, medicine and the professions. At the time of the Watergate crisis, for example, it was disclosed that this was the faith that pervaded the legal profession. The influence of Descartes, and his admirers, is clearly seen in the opinion of Roscoe Pound when he states in his first volume of *Jurisprudence* that "everything in the law had to be rested upon reason and upon reason only."

Christianity's influence upon the optimistic view of nature.

I referred to Aldous Huxley's faith as a model of the optimism upheld by many humanists. Its presumption is common to the variety of expressions which end with an "ism." The reason for such optimism according to

Huxley is, "Man is that part of reality in which and through which the cosmic process has become conscious and has begun to comprehend itself." We are now, it may be presumed, involved in the psychological evolution which will lead mankind on to the happy day when there will be peace, pleasure and freedom for all. This plateau is inevitable, for the process of convergence must make for the integration of everyone into a single world society. Huxley does not trouble to question the desirability of such an end. He is confident that it is the ultimate good.

I wonder if this optimism would be possible without the Christian faith. I do not think so. What is ignored in this optimism is the revelation, to which the Bible witnesses. The world as we know it is neither illusion nor chemical accident. It is God's by intention, purpose, creation and redemption. Because it has a beginning and an end, because creation implies time and space, and because the nature of its goal has been revealed in Jesus Christ, we have hope; that is, we apprehend by faith the good end God has prepared for those who love Him. Very briefly, let us look at three basic views of time.

There is the *classical Greek* and *Oriental* one, which believes that time is a wheel of birth, life and decay. All change, therefore, is cyclical. As things have been, so will they be again. If there is progress, there is also regression. Indeed, according to Professor Stanley Jaki in his book, *Science and Creation*, it is this emphasis on regression that dominates. This results in despair, and a pessimistic view of human beings and nature.

In Jesus' day the prevailing view was that time and creation proceeded from the beginning, when God spoke His creative Word, to the Last Day, when the history of mankind would be rolled into one and judged. Martha and Nicodemus expressed this linear conception of time in their conversations with Jesus. Such a view implies the idea of progress and development. Its influence on Western thought is obvious. But is not this the Christian view as well? Not quite! Christ makes the difference. In Him, and through Him, we know the beginning and the end. He is the summing up of mankind and creation as the second Adam, the Son of man. Through Him, God has acted. Both space and time are transcended through His presence in the flesh. All time flows to Him, and from Him. The place where time and eternity, sin and holiness, man and God meet is the cross. The crucifixion of our Lord is both the completion of His incarnation and the beginning of the new age. This new age is the fulfillment of creation. In recognition of this, we as Christians celebrate the New Covenant (2 Cor. 3:6); the new Sabbath—Sunday instead of Saturday—as the day of freedom and new life; and the new people of God of which Pentecost is the testimony (Rom. 8:9-30).

Another name for the Christian view of time is *salvation history.* It is God in Christ, who gives purpose and, therefore, meaning to history. Without the revelation of God in Christ, history has no meaning, nor purpose, nor destiny, nor completion. The best summing up of this salvation history is to be found in Stephen's address to the high priest in Acts 7. Beginning with Abraham, Stephen shows how it was God who called His people into being. Having founded His people in a miraculous way by the birth of Isaac, God gave the rite of circumcision to Abraham as a sign of the covenant. By the call of Moses, God liberated His people from the prison compounds of Egypt, and sustained them in the wilderness. Although Moses received God's personal revelation, his people refused to obey him. Stephen pointed out that Caiaphas and his followers were like the people of old who refused to obey God. The terrible consequence of this disobedience was that the Holy Spirit had been resisted; and Jesus, God's righteous servant, had been murdered, as were the prophets in past days. For this witness, Stephen was stoned to death, thus indicating the continuing disobedience of people to God's ultimate revelation. To read and reflect upon Stephen's spoken and acted witness is to be aware that it is the history of all people in their disobedience, and also the history of God in His steadfast love.

In salvation history we see how the revealing power of God continuously transcends the linear process of time from, and time to. In Christ, history has been fulfilled and made meaningful. My existence today is significant because the salvation of God in Christ is mine to claim now. Having claimed it, as St. Paul reminded the Philippians, I am to work it out in "fear and trembling" (Phil. 2:12). To work it out, of course, implies completing it in the freedom that salvation has made possible.

As Christians, all of us may say boldly it is the Christian faith which provided an optimistic outlook for history. As I have suggested, the theory upheld by non-Christian civilizations was one which was uniformly pessimistic. Because of their pessimistic faith, there was no hope of a new beginning, or of God's active presence within creation. These non-Christian views had no concept of hope. St. Paul has emphasized this truth in these words: "Remember that you were at that time separated from Christ, alienated from the commonwealth of Israel, and strangers to the covenants of promise, having no hope and without God in the world" (Eph. 2:12 RSV). This reference to their despair in their past experience in the godless world was obviously something the Ephesians understood only too well. Having stressed the optimism of our faith, it is essential to remember that this optimism has its setting in the secular time of Caesars, tyrants, governments, taxation, war, racism and poverty. Does not this mean for us that salvation is now in the time of our mortal existence, and that the limitations of secular time are daily transcended by the action of grace? We may affirm accordingly that secular time is subject to the Creator/Redeemer and His time, the time of salvation and grace.

This practical analysis of secular time saves us from the false, and at times, arrogant Utopianism of the secular faith. Yes, we know there is a good end for us and all God's people, but this is in God's time. Meanwhile, we live in the time of grace and journey toward its fulfillment in glory.

One of the best critiques I know of the belief in progress and its optimistic goal is that of Karl Löwith in his important, but little known, book, *Meaning in History*. His thesis is that history alone cannot prove the existence, or non-existence, of God; nor can it provide its own meaning. He demonstrates that every contemporary view of history which claims to see meaning, purpose, progress and process in history is both fallacious and a poor imitation of salvation history. His conclusion is so important that I shall quote a section from it in length:

> Radical atheism, too, which is, however, as rare as radical faith, is possible only within a Christian tradition; for the feeling that the world is thoroughly godless and godforsaken presupposes

the belief in a transcendent Creator-God who cares for his creatures.

He goes on to point out that the Christian faith affirmed God as distinct from the world as Creator, yet, at the same time being the source of all that is. Once this faith is rejected,

> . . . there remains only one aspect: the sheer contingency of its mere "existence." The post-Christian world is a creation without creator, and a *saeculum* (in the ecclesiastical sense of this term) turned secular for lack of religious perspective. . . . Is it perhaps Jewish Messianism and secular eschatology, though in their secular transformations, that have developed those appalling energies of creative activity which changed the Christian Occident into a world-wide civilization? It was certainly not a pagan but a Christian culture which brought about this revolution. The ideal of modern science of mastering the forces of nature and the idea of progress emerged neither in the classical world nor in the East, but in the West. But what enabled us to remake the world in the image of man? Is it perhaps that the belief in being created in the image of a Creator-God, the hope in a future Kingdom of God, and the Christian command to spread the gospel to all nations for the sake of salvation have turned into the secular presumption that we have to transform the world into a better world in the image of man and to save unregenerate nations by westernization and re-education? *(Meaning in History)*

The more we analyze the various expressions of secular humanism, the more we see that they are nothing but a cheap counterfeit of the Christian faith. When we see them as this, we are in a better position to explain the gospel as it is in its depth and breadth. A mere reaction to such counterfeits is of little help. Instead of raging against Marxist Leninism, for example, Christians would be wiser to understand the intellectual vitality of the gospel and its historical expression in the consciousness of Christ's community. If Marxism is a counterfeit, is it not better to point to the real thing? Yes, we may say reality is dynamic. Yes, change is taking place all the time; remember that our Lord healed on the Sabbath. Because it was the Lord's day of freedom and healing, the Sabbath is made for man. Yes, there is continuous creation in the sense that God has not left His universe to the mercy of our theories. He cares for His world, and every individual at every time. Remember Jesus died for the world God loved. Remember as well that the God we trust is ever active. Because Jesus demonstrated this, He was crucified. In justification for His healing miracles on the Sabbath, Jesus told His accusers: "My Father is working still, and I am working" (John 5:17). It is this faith that makes the difference. The difference is one of optimism and joy. That is why humanism, when it is left to itself without the benefits of the Christian faith, very quickly loses its optimism.

4

The Despair of Humanism

Once the humanist finds there is no meaning in the universe—that individuals are stripped of their unique consciousness because of the control of the secular consciousness of the collective society, and that consciousness is an illusion—there is not much left in which to believe. This is the condition of despair. Humanists have been, and are, aware of this condition. If we liked, we could trace this awareness of despair back to the so-called halcyon days of the romantics, namely, the days of classical Greece. For example, this line from Theognis, "The best of all things for earthly men is not to be born. . . ." But, instead, we shall look briefly at the modern period of the post-Renaissance.

In my first chapter, I referred to the Tower of Babel as a symbol of godless civilization. Its citizens' pride brought about its fall, and the subsequent confusion. No one understood another, and no one cared. It is a prophetic description of contemporary humanist society. A humanist who seemed to be aware of this plight was Thomas Hobbes (1588-1679). He was still close enough to Christian thought to conceive of an orderly universe. Within this order he believed there existed the law of happiness. This law was the key to the establishment of an orderly society, such as that of

James I, of the United Kingdom of England and Scotland. He presumed that everyone would seek his or her own happiness—on the basis that people are naturally directed either to the preservation of life, or to the heightening of its pleasures. Because the monarch held the power of life and death over his subjects, i.e., the power to take a life for disobedience, the obvious thing for the subject to do was to obey the monarch's laws and enjoy his rewards. B.F. Skinner's theory of positive reinforcement may be seen as a projection of this "obvious truth."

Hobbes realized that the rejection of the divine revelation results in amoral existence—an existence in which there is neither right nor wrong, good nor sin, freedom nor responsibility, salvation nor judgment. He outlines the human predicament thus, "Every man calleth that which pleaseth him good; and that which displeaseth him evil." How can any stable society survive when the only authority is that of the whims, fancies and pleasures of each individual? Obviously it cannot, reasoned Hobbes. His answer was that of investing authority in the monarch, who had the power of death, to intimidate, and thus, control this otherwise anarchical and chaotic situation. This kind of thinking must have reinforced the theory of monarchical absolutism so dear to the heart of the House of Stuart, as well as reinforcing materialism of the kind that may be designated as "matter on the move."

In this theory, we see the beginning of tyranny, and the dawn of the collective or controlled consciousness. It is a prefiguring of what happened in Nazi Germany, and in Russia. A contemporary answer to this problem, as it is stated by intellectuals, is the "*as if*" answer. According to this solution, we are to recognize that no absolute moral authority exists. What we have to do, therefore, in this moral vacuum, is to decide and act *as if* it does exist. One of the most cogent advocates of this position—or non-position—is Arthur Koestler. I rate him as one of the liveliest intellects in the present literary scene. He has won the right to be considered thus because of his experiences. His life story is that of the plight of the intellectual in modern society. He was brought up and educated in Austria. As a Jew he became fascinated with the Zionist movement. Shortly before his final examinations for a degree in engineering he left for Israel to take part in the struggle of the Zionists for a homeland. This did not satisfy him so he turned to Communism. He became an international agent with the responsibility of initiating strikes and revolts in western Europe. So efficient was he in his task that he was rewarded with an all-expenses-paid trip to Russia. What he saw there displeased him. In the collective society of the Soviet Union, everyday existence had been reduced to monotonous boredom. It was Dullsville, Incorporated.

As part of his discipline in thinking his way out of Communism, he wrote a trilogy of novels. In the first, *The Gladiators*, he came to the conclusion that it is impossible to found an ideal society without a moral absolute. The gladiators, in their attempts to establish their Sun State, ended up by becoming like Rome. Thus, they were destroyed by the authority against which they had rebelled. What was missing was a moral core similar to that contained in the Sermon on the Mount. The second novel is well known: *Darkness at Noon*. In this he shows us the revolutionary commissar who becomes lost in "the law of detours," and is destroyed by it. "The law of detours" is the law which declares that when the State is the only absolute, then only that which maintains the power of the State is acceptable. For comrades/citizens there are only means, including people, and these means are determined by what is expedient for the State. Because the commissar was unable to realize this law, he was executed by the State he had tried to serve, and thus he was relegated to the garbage heap of meaningless means.

The third novel is *Arrival and Departure*. It is probably the most autobiographical of the three. The story is of a revolutionary who had been captured and imprisoned, but who escaped to a country that is neutral during World War II. While he waits for a ship to take him to the United States, he has an affair with a refugee psychiatrist. She sleeps with him, and psychoanalyzes him. Both of these experiences are presumed to produce happiness. When the psychiatrist leaves him on an earlier ship, she assures him he no longer needs to worry about his old moral hang-ups. He has been liberated for happiness, which will be fulfilled for both of them in the country of happiness—the United States of America.

The revolutionary's ship arrives. He boards it, and puts his luggage in his cabin. The way to happiness is now clear and assured. But the revolutionary abandons the ship. He realizes a man cannot live by happiness alone. To be human he has to make a moral decision. The last scene is that of the revolutionary parachuting into the country from which he had escaped. The symbolism is clear: he has to be involved in the moral struggle, no matter how costly it may be. He has to live *as if* there were a moral demand made of him.

The tragedy of Arthur Koestler, and his fellow intellectuals, is that he recognizes the need for moral commitment, a commitment which transcends one that may be expected by the secular state of its subjects. Koestler finds that this kind of commitment is still possible within the free countries of the West. So far as I can judge, however, he fails to realize that there can be only one source of absolute moral demand, and that is, of course, God.

Both Hobbes and Koestler end up by showing that the optimism of humanism is merely a euphemism for despair.

Although David Hume (1711-1776) is commonly regarded as a skeptic of religion, which he was, he was also a skeptic of humanism. He pointed out that rational methods are as limited as reason itself. If there is nothing to which one may commit oneself, then there is no possibility of the conviction necessary for moral action. He wrote, "Reason is no motive to action except so far as it directs the impulse received from appetite or inclination." Thus there is no guarantee that our appetites and desires will direct or motivate us even to preserve our own skins as Hobbes had presumed. Indeed, there is no reason to presume that we shall try to preserve our own existence when our desires are frustrated. The opposite is often the case. Freud touches upon this in his teaching on *thanatos*, the death wish, which has been ignored, for the most part, by his disciples.

Thomas G. Masaryk, the first president of liberated Czechoslovakia after World War I, was a Christian social philosopher as well as a politician. The thesis of his book, *Suicide and the Meaning of Civilization*, is that the more godless a society becomes, the greater the number of suicides. In the Middle Ages, the number of suicides was negligible. By the end of the nineteenth century, suicide was rated as one of the top causes of death, and the vast majority of these deaths occurred among highly principled humanists. This seems to be the tragic story of moral individuals who have no moral resources beyond themselves. Their principled morality is one of humanist law.

In one of his essays, Robert Louis Stevenson tells of an experience he had while on a walking holiday in the county of Fife in Scotland. He stopped to watch a farm laborer mucking the byre. While he watched the man at his task, he discoursed with him on a number of subjects including philosophy, literature and religion. The range of the man's interests impressed Stevenson. He asked him why he could work at such a menial task and yet have such enjoyment of life. His response illustrates my point: "He that has something ayond him need never be weary." Those who have nothing beyond them, on the other hand, are weary with the weariness of despair.

Unyielding Despair

In the third chapter, I referred to Julian Huxley's faith in the inevitable progress of the cosmic process. So great was his faith that he could describe evolutionary humanism as the new religion for the scientific age and mind. After reading his book, *Evolutionary Humanism,* Bertrand Russell commented that such an optimism required a faith greater than that demanded of Christians.

Russell, an Englishman of a distinguished and comparatively affluent family, analyzed the optimism of humanism as that of unyielding despair. This passage from *A Free Man's Worship* should be remembered:

That Man is the product of causes which had no prevision of the end they were achieving; that his

origin, his growth, his hopes and fears, his loves
and his beliefs, are but the outcome of accidental
collocations of atoms; that no fire, no heroism, no
intensity of thought and feeling can preserve an
individual life beyond the grave; that all the labor
of the ages, all the devotion, all the inspiration, all
the noon-day brightness of human genius, are
destined to extinction in the vast death of the solar
system, and that the whole temple of Man's
achievements must inevitably be buried beneath
the debris of a universe in ruins—all these things,
if not quite beyond dispute, are yet so nearly
certain, that no philosophy which rejects them can
hope to stand. Only within the scaffolding of these
truths, only on the firm foundation of unyielding
despair, can the soul's habitation henceforth be
safely built.

Few humanists are as brave as Lord Russell. Yet it
is this unyielding despair that prevails. What Walter
Lippman called "the acids of modernity" have eroded
the optimism of nineteenth-century humanism. The
elements of despair within it have come to the fore to
dominate the feelings of society as a whole. The
evidences of unyielding despair were obvious in
Europe, particularly after World War I. The United
States is, perhaps, the last resort of this now old-
fashioned optimism. The last evidences of this still
hang around in the atmosphere of most universities,
but usually only in the thinking of those who have not
read sufficient history.

It is important to remember also that it is woven into
the fabric of American religious thought, particularly
on the part of those who think they have escaped from
the blight of original sin. When I came to the United

States from Scotland, I was astonished to learn of highly popular preachers who advocated faith as a means to success—the American goal. Presumably anyone with enough faith could make a million. A few of those preachers demonstrated the efficacy of their own faith by achieving their million-dollar destiny.

In case you may think I am being blasphemous, let me say that I found my faith in Jesus as Lord dissuaded me from attempting to make a million. Indeed, what small success I ever had in the economic field had nothing to do with my Christian faith, only with my faith in myself. And is not this merely my original sin? What is more, the very brave men of faith in Christ, who introduced me to their Lord, achieved no worldly success. The bravest and kindest man I have known was crucified for being so good that He threatened His enemies. Nowhere in the New Testament are we promised worldly success. From what I know, the Christian faith is one of, and for, failures. It begins with a failure: Jesus Christ. And it continues with failures. I do not recall either Jesus, or His disciples, trying to become a Caesar. What a vast difference there is between the latter symbol and that of the cross! The despair of human existence, which usually begins in human optimism, is transcended by Christ's victory on the cross, and all that it implies. Christ's kingdom is not of this world; because it is not, it triumphs.

The story of man, as it is evaluated in the literature of humanism all the way from Homer to today, is the literature of despair. It is the story which ends in spiritual failure. Earlier I wrote that the irrationality of reason resulted in romanticism. I now go on to say that the irrationalism of romanticism results in the despair of atheistic existentialism. Sartre, as the chief spokesman of this cult of despair, tells us that we are cast into the prison cell of freedom where we have to create our own essence or meaning. In his book, *Intimacies*, he outlines a series of perversions as if to say that the best we can do in our freedom is to rebel against acceptable standards of conduct. Thus, perversions are acts of our freedom. But, when perversions are acceptable, what do we do with our freedom? Does not this seem to be the developing situation in our society? In his book, *Nausea*, Sartre paints a picture of an undistinguished man who shudders every time he looks into the mirror and sees himself. Thus, humanism ends up by being nothing but the reflection of ourselves.

A few years ago while I was visiting Sweden, I spent some time with a Lutheran pastor. When I met him at his home, he told me he had just come from the funeral of a twenty-one-year-old student. "How did he die?" I asked.

"By his own hand. Suicide!"

"Why?"

"He didn't know what to do with his freedom."

This may be the tragic picture of those in the godless society who have nothing to do with their freedom but to despair—and die. This is, in effect, what the humanist existentialists are telling us. Without God all things are possible, but without God our attempts to do all things result in failure, defeat, despair, death. Is not this the point made repeatedly by Camus? Our freedom leads us to the death cell, the city under plague, the alienation of the exile in a foreign land as the witness, or forerunner, of nothing.

I find it interesting that those who write to inform us that there is no God, no meaning and only despair, nevertheless keep writing about it as though they hoped to find meaning in their activity. But even this quality of unyielding despair becomes yielding despair. Those of you who have read Samuel Beckett's novels, or seen his play, *Waiting for Godot*, will recall how he exposes us to the futility of our existence because there is no meaning in it. There cannot be, because there is nothing but nothing. This is what our freedom to do what we please means—nothing.

Samuel Beckett, once the secretary of James Joyce, not only wrote about yielding despair but demonstrated it in his own experience. On the completion of his novel, *The Unnamable*, he stated, "The work brought me to the point where I felt I was saying the same thing over and over again. For some authors writing gets easier the more they write. For me it gets more and more difficult. For the area of possibilities gets smaller and smaller and smaller. At the end of my work there is nothing but dust. . . . In the last book there is complete disintegration. No 'I,' no 'being.' No nominative, no accusative, no verbs. There is no way to go on."

It is interesting how the belief that says, "I can do all things because everything is possible for me" is reduced to smaller and smaller possibilities. How quickly the questionable optimism of "unyielding despair" becomes so quickly the pessimism of yielding despair.

One of the most sensitive appreciations of this condition was contained in an article written for *The Atlantic Monthly* in 1951, by Walter Stace, late professor of philosophy at Princeton University. It was entitled, "Man Against Darkness." He began his essay by referring to a statement made by the Catholic Bishops of America deploring the loss of Christian faith in the country. Although he confessed to have no religion, he agreed with the bishops. He referred to Jean-Paul Sartre as being in agreement, for he, too, had taught that "the world which surrounds us is nothing but an immense spiritual emptiness." He also referred to Bertrand Russell's statement in *A Free Man's Worship*. Russell, he observed, was unduly critical of religion. Whatever its faults, it had saved human beings from the calamity of despair. For Russell, therefore, to count its disappearance as a blessing was absurd.

On the other hand, it is equally absurd for humanists to live as though the world will go on as before without God. He points out, as I am doing, that: "The root cause of the decay of faith has not been any particular discovery of science, but rather the general spirit of science and certain basic assumptions upon which modern science, from the seventeenth century onwards, has proceeded." The true cause, Stace wrote, was the rejection of the belief in cosmic order and purpose. Once the conception of purpose in the world was frowned upon, the way was prepared for the denial of God. The denial of God results in the denial of human beings. Nature is nothing but matter in motion without a purpose.

I agree with Stace that it is this emphasis upon *purposelessness* that is the keystone of despair, and not the teaching that the sun, not the earth, is the center of our planetary system; nor the fact that the earth is hundreds of millions of years old; nor the unprovable assumption that we are descended from the missing link, our simian ancestor. It is the theme of purposelessness which replaces that of moral order, creation by God, our origin and destiny. According to this theme, both Jesus' teaching on the kingdom of God and Kant's emphasis in the kingdom of ends in which reason reigns are replaced by the kingdom of futility. No matter what we may do, our lives remain hollow at the center. "Hence the dissatisfied, disillusioned, restless spirit of modern man." We might well wonder why it is that the scientists pursue their research and inquiries. Why investigate what was once called the natural order, and why bother to teach science, when "belief in the ultimate irrationality of everything is the quintessence of what is called the modern mind"? This is the kind of question that most universities are afraid to ask. Perhaps, if they did, they would lose the support of their wealthy alumni or alumnae. Or, if they are controlled by governments, they are merely technocratic processing plants for the production of bureaucrats. And, therefore, they do not trouble to ask the question about their purpose.

While I am writing this chapter, I find myself forced by the events of our times to conclude that the plight of most universities is one of moral absurdity. Why? Because there is no viable reason for their existence except as processing plants. When there is neither right nor wrong, why ask senseless questions about the rightness of historical, social and political events? Why expect students not to cheat in examinations, or faculty in experiments, if there is no point to academic endeavors? The picture that develops in my mind is that of an enormous fishbowl in which a variety of blank-eyed fish swim around aimlessly breaking the boredom once in a while by eating one another.

I appreciate Walter Stace's honest analysis of our intellectual predicament, which he sums up as follows: "Along with the ruin of the religious vision, there went the ruin of moral principles and indeed of all values. If there is a cosmic purpose, if there is in the nature of things a drive towards goodness, then our moral systems will derive their validity from this. But if our moral rules do not proceed from something outside us in the nature of the universe—whether we say it is God or simply the universe itself—then they must be our own inventions.

"Thus it came to be believed that moral rules must be merely an expression of our own likes and dislikes. But likes and dislikes are notoriously variable. What pleases one man, people, or culture, displeases another. Therefore morals are wholly relative." To this truth, our contemporary moral expressions testify strongly. And nowhere is ethical relativity practiced more unquestioningly than among politicians, philosophers, sociologists, educators, corporation presidents, and academic administrators of massive educational process plants sometimes erroneously designated as universities. As C.S. Lewis pointed out in his *Men Without Chests*, such institutions teach that we are the pawns of genetic and environmental processes, and therefore, we are not responsible for our actions; yet whenever students demonstrate this ethical relativism, the advocates complain of it bitterly.

A few years ago, I was asked to speak at a conference of psychiatrists on the subject of the religious and moral experience, because administrators kept sending them students with religious/moral problems. This was done on the presumption that psychiatrists were behavioral engineers who could correct the technical malfunctions of those who did not respond as expected to the technical process.

The essentially pessimistic quality of Walter Stace's article is considerably reinforced by his conclusion; and an honest one it is. He points out that "no civilization can live without ideals, or to put it in another way, without a firm faith in moral ideas. Our ideals and moral ideas have in the past been rooted in religion. . . . It would therefore look as if the early death of our civilization were inevitable." Many European philosophers have been saying the same thing for the past sixty years. What folly it is, therefore, for humanists to exist like ostriches with their heads in the sand. Yet, this is the situation of intellectuals who refuse to recognize the conclusion of their own miserable premises: the product of their yielding to despair.

The despair of Walter Stace's "unfaith" is honestly stated: "To be genuinely civilized means to be able to walk straightly and to live honorably without the props and crutches of one or another of the childish dreams which have so far supported men. That such a life is likely to be ecstatically happy I will not claim." If people do not learn to live heroically with this despair they will "sink back into the savagery and brutality" from which they once are presumed to have emerged. Indeed, what else might one expect if there is *only* the faith of humanism with its origin and ending in despair.

Personally, I find it intriguing to note that prophets of despair still find time to declare it; that professors continue to teach it; that scientists pursue exacting research with no hope of disproving it; and that universities still waste enormous sums of money in its service.

I would expect that a humanist's response to my criticism would run something like this: "You see humanism from the position of the Christian faith; thus, for you humanism is nothing but a sum of subtraction. Subtract spirit or soul, sin, origin and destiny, Jesus Christ and God, and nothing remains but death and despair. Humanists do not think this way. We do not begin by presuming that God is in his heavens, therefore, everything is all right. We begin where we are, and 'create the world we live in by our expectations and attitudes, our ideals and ideas, and the ways in which we manage our experience.' We create our own possibilities for better or worse. We accept the responsibility for our own fate. Is not this morality enough? Our experiences confirm that we are the ones who originate them, and no one else. What you, as a Christian, classify as faith, I, as a humanist, classify as a confidence in the human ability to design one's own life styles. Although civilizations fall, they also rise. And they rise because of those who, in their time, develop the art of living. Civilization is the visible expression of this art."

And I would answer, "Quite!"

On an examination of the humanist's faith, I am inclined to presume it is not as central to his actions as he would like to believe; nor that his despair is as genuine as his logic claims it to be. His little faith is, perhaps, protected by that greater faith centered upon the God/man, Jesus. My presumption does not surprise me: for it is this greater faith that initiated the intellectual dynamic of Western civilization, and preserved it from the unyielding despair of the law of endless recurrence, which blighted the bud of intellectual possibilities in previous civilizations. Where there is no vision, or moral authority, such as that provided by faith in Christ, then the people perish.

Professor Trevor-Roper, the English historian, wrote in his book, *The Rise of Christian Europe*, in the conviction that, "The history of the past may help us to explain . . . the vitality of western civilization." The faith of despairing humanism may be at its rope's end, and dragging in the polluted mud of twentieth-century misery, but the Christian faith still awaits to be tried and proved victorious. It has experienced many deaths, but it is the last resurrection, however, that counts.

A scientist, Dr. Robert E. Clark, of Cambridge, tells us in his analysis of science, and the spectacular contributions of scientists of faith, that "Intellectually, there is no royal road to discovery. Whether scientific or religious, it involves risk and passionate faith" *(Science and Christianity: A Partnership)*. Dr. Clark gives several examples of scientists who continued their research in the face of opposition on the part of their scientific fraternity purely on the strength of their faith in God. Faraday, for example, pursued his research in the belief that there is an underlying unity and order in nature, because it is the creation of God who is one (i.e., the one and only I AM).

The point has to be made by Christians that Christianity does not reject science as some humanists may claim. On the contrary, it creates the faith that makes authentic scientific investigation possible. The Bible is true, and because it is, it demands that we use our intelligence in every area. The greater our faith, the more we may want to learn of the ways of our Creator in nature, as well as in all of our relationships, which, of course, are beyond the range of scientific measurement. The one we name Lord is Lord because He is the truth.

5

Why Go to University?

By this time you may feel like asking the question: Why go to university? If the ethos on campus is critical of the Christian faith, why should I risk my faith?

The first answer is a simple, yet basic, one. We cannot be Christians in a vacuum. If we cannot risk our faith, it may be time to question its authenticity. Jesus never promised His disciples security. Read again His High Priestly Prayer recorded in John 17. Jesus states that His Father gave Him the disciples *out of the world*, and that He is leaving them *in the world*. He does not pray that they be taken *out of the world*, but that they may be kept safe from the evil one. The reason for being *in the world* is clear. It is to witness for Him. Thus, Jesus prays not only for them, but for those who will become disciples in response to the first disciples' witness in the world.

We are right to view the campus scene as an opportunity for witness. I believe the university is one of the primary fields of mission in our times. Yet, it is also a place of preparation for witness in the world. It offers you a variety of opportunities. Among these are the privileges associated with your involvement in a variety of disciplines that afford you the means of attaining your freedom to be an artist, nurse, doctor, physicist, chemist, mathematician, musician, dramatist, accountant, banker, lawyer, judge, engineer, geologist, ecologist, architect, teacher or whatever.

It is important to realize the university is not against you, but for you. You are not compelled to attend it. You choose to do so. You choose the discipline that will free you to be the professional person capable of taking his or her place in the world. Our vocation is to be Christians wherever we are. Our education, therefore, is a tool to be used in our calling.

The second answer to the question concerning a university education is that usually universities help us to be better prepared for living in the world and serving Jesus as Lord. This is increasingly true in an age when only a few have the privilege of being farmers, or shepherds, or fishermen, or masons. The complexities of modern society have resulted in a different marketplace: a technological, and service-oriented, one.

While I was walking home from campus one afternoon, I noticed a friend of mine limping along the pathway. I greeted him. He turned to me. I knew by his face that his limp was more than the consequence of a simple accident. His face was badly twisted to one side. When he returned my greeting, his voice was slurred, so slurred that I had the greatest difficulty in understanding what he was saying. It was a plea for help.

"Ernest, I'm in a bad way. Tumor in the brain. I'm off to hospital in Philadelphia tomorrow. Pray for me. Give me a text." The ones that flashed into my mind were: "He is not God of the dead, but of the living" (Matt. 22:32 RSV), and "Do not be anxious about tomorrow, for tomorrow will be anxious for itself" (Matt. 6:34 RSV).

About six weeks later, I received a long, rambling letter from him. He wrote: "I thanked the surgeon for the operation. He replied, 'Don't thank me; thank God. Your tumor was a bad one. My colleagues advised me to let it go. I decided to operate. So I prayed: told God I didn't know what was there. Then I put my hands into God's hands, and He did the rest.' So here I am, a Jew thanking God and two Christians for saving my life. You for praying for me, and the surgeon for operating. Strange are the ways of the Lord."

As Christians in the world, this is what we do; we put ourselves—our talents, our gifts, our intelligence, our education—into God's hands and let Him do the rest. He respects the best we offer Him and uses it for His glory and the well-being of His people.

It was not universities that created Christians, but it was Christians who founded universities. They did so because they needed places to grow and learn. We may say that the universities in the West were the projection of the Christian community. The study of languages, literature, mathematics, physics, astronomy, music, art, theology and philosophy occurred in Christian communities which formed the pattern for universities. Some people may regard this origin as being too humble. Those who do so usually presume it was governments and scientific societies that were the initiators. This is true of later secular universities, but not of the early ones. Those provided the model and forms. Hence the absurdity at commencement time of humanists dressed up to look like medieval monks or Reformed scholars.

Education and Culture

While most of us think of education in terms of the professional goals we have for ourselves, we also think of it as a means of improving our minds and our understanding. Thus, on the one hand we perceive it as a good

77

and necessary discipline, and on the other, as a means
of personal satisfaction. We are offered both the view
of an expanding external macrocosm, and the view of a
deepening microcosm. Through the discipline of the
sciences we are able to realize more of the variety,
complexity, integrity and wonder of the created cosmos. Such an understanding, however, requires faith
in the Creator. When the Psalmist proclaims, "The
heavens declare the glory of God" (Ps. 19:1), he is imply-
ing more than a knowledge of the metagalaxies through
the study of astronomy. That something more is that
inner quality we classify as faith. How do the heavens
declare the glory of God if you do not believe in Him?
Delight in the glory and wonder of creation is not the
work of the heavens, but the response of the believers
to their Creator. One who is an authentic humanist
may observe and measure the metagalaxies, but only
the believer sees the glory of God through the eyes of
faith. The difference between these two points of perception is aptly expressed by Elizabeth Barrett Browning
in a stanza from "Aurora Leigh":

Earth's crammed with heaven,
And every common bush afire with God;
But only he who sees, takes off his shoes,
The rest sit round it and pluck blackberries,
And daub their natural face unaware
More and more from the first similitude.

It is this vision of the divine *shekinah* (glory) that
makes all the difference. This difference is easily perceived in terms of a purposeless, or purposeful, universe. Which raises again the very pertinent question:
What purpose is there for a university in a purposeless
universe? Against the negation of humanism is the
resounding "yes" of the Christian faith: the faith that

caused universities to come into being, because they had a purpose in a purposeful universe.

The inner life of faith is nurtured by the study of culture. Here we may define culture as the outward signs of invisible grace. The culture of the West is Christian in origin. That is, this is the norm from which the humanist deviates. It was initiated by Jesus, and articulated by His believing followers. The form of the articulation was the community of believers and the New Testament, or New Covenant. If you look at the seals of the first colleges in the United States, you will see that the Bible dominates as the visible expression of the colleges' origin and purpose.

The people of the Book founded their colleges as communities of Christians in which the Bible and its varied dependent cultural offshoots could be studied. The Bible is basic. It is the literary evidence of God's revelation. It is true! Because it is, we need not be afraid of subjecting it to the most critical scrutiny. Its position today is stronger than ever. Scholarship has not weakened it. On the contrary, it has emphasized its uniqueness. Our approach to it, therefore, should not be the acceptance of it as a magical book, or as a laboratory record of scientific data, but the recognition that it is the historical account of God's mighty acts. The revelation that is incomplete in the Old Covenant is complete in the New. We have the evidence that "the Word became flesh and dwelt among us" (John 1:1). The First Letter of St. John states this clearly, "That which was from the beginning, which we have heard, which we have seen with our eyes, which we have looked upon, and our hands have handled, of the Word of life" (1 John 1:1).

This great declaration marks the dividing line between the Jew and the Christian. For the former, the divine revelation is limited to the Torah; for the latter it is centered upon the man Jesus. Note, however, that in both cases the revelation is external. For the Jew it is the Torah given to Moses at Mount Sinai. For the Christian it is Jesus, crucified, raised from the dead and exalted by God's power. These are the objective facts that call their respective faiths into being. These faiths do not depend upon a subjective anthropological theory so dear to the thinking of humanists. They are the response to a given and objective revelation.

With this background, we are able to have a better understanding of Christian culture as the "spin off" of the Bible and its study. The Bible is still the book above all books that originates all great thoughts and lofty actions. Above all, it sustains the lively memory of Jesus, who is the truth by whom we live. In living this truth, His followers create culture. Within this Christian culture, we have a unique understanding of creation and its ways; we have a vital philosophy, a high ethic, humane laws, human art, the humanities, the sciences and our various social and political systems.

Those of you who are familiar with the writings of Francis A. Schaeffer will be familiar with his criticisms of contemporary humanism, and his advocacy of a truly spiritual culture centered in Jesus as Lord of all, including the mind and its cultural manifestations.

Sir Llewellyn Woodward reminded his fellow Fellows, at All Souls College, Oxford, in June, 1969, of this truth in these words: "The Christian message cannot be watered down into a general 'get-togetherness'; it is not a formula or gadget for relieving the dullness of life on housing estates. The *new way* of the Christians held what in modern jargon is termed the social environment to be evil beyond remedy; it described all men as sinners alienated from God by their own choice as well

as by their inheritance, and called them to repent."
After challenging the secular faith by this reference to
Christianity's uniqueness, he went on to emphasize a
point I have made previously, namely that the rejection
of the revealed religion results in despair. "The aban-
donment of religious belief is not accompanied by
increased demonstrations of joy. The astonishing rele-
vance to our case of so much in the writings of the
Hebrew prophets leads me to quote from one of them:
'The earth mourneth and fadeth away. . . . The in-
habitants of the earth are burned, and few men left.
. . . The new wine mourneth, the vine languisheth, all
the merryhearted do sigh. . . . The noise of them that
rejoice endeth, the joy of the harp ceaseth. . . . The
city of confusion is broken down' " (Isa. 24:4-10).

Such scholars are urging their fellow Christians to
challenge the dominance of the secular culture in the
name of Christ; and for the sake of a vital Christian
culture in which each individual is encouraged to
achieve his or her total maturity by commitment to
Jesus as Lord; and to the service of His brothers and
sisters. In this challenge there is respect for the university as an island of culture with a role yet to be
fulfilled. Undergirding such a position is again the
recognition that it is not given to the positive sciences
to confront ultimate reality. This is given to the Christian faith alone. Science is an essential exercise of our
intellects, but faith is the pledge and involvement of
our whole selves, wills, emotions and intelligence. Just
as it takes the Church, as the Body of Christ, to respond
totally to God's revelation of himself, so does it take a
university, in the totality of its disciplines and existence, to respond to the complexity of God's world and
His Word. This is an awesome task which may be fulfilled only in the humility of the Christian faith.

Christianity and Culture

The danger we must look out for is that of deifying, or belittling culture. The pride of humanism is that of placing culture in the throne that rightly belongs to God and His Son. By the nineteenth century, the humanists had rejected God in their belief that man, that is, the universal idea of man, is God. Because the emphasis was upon the universal idea, "man" was translated into culture. Individuals were its products, and ultimately its slaves. The German adoration of *Kultur* contributed to the rise of Hitler and the demonic madness of the Third Reich. All of us have been influenced by it. As one of the idols of this passing age, it has spawned every form of socialism, and nurtured the bureaucracy of the state and multi-national corporations.

The deification of culture has influenced religious thinkers of both the right and the left, those, that is, who have put the supremacy of their cultural obsessions above the lordship of Jesus Christ. He is subject to no culture; for, as Francis A. Schaeffer claims rightly, he is the Lord of culture.

To deny, or belittle culture, on the other hand, is to be out of our minds. As Christians in the world, we have bodies shaped by natural processes, and minds influenced by our culture—that of the West. I was conscious of this when I went to Asia as a young man. Asiatics thought differently and upheld different values. For one thing, the external world of observable phenomena was regarded as *maya*, illusion—the shadow, that is, of the imagined reality. And for another, individuals had no specific worth or dignity. Once, when my infantry company was supervising the cleaning of an arsenal by an Asiatic labor force, a laborer picked up a loose Mill's hand grenade, and held it to his ear to see if it ticked. His comrades pantomimed to him to pull out the pin. He did and held it to his ear again while the others rushed to the nearby monsoon drain for cover. Needless to say, the grenade exploded and blew his head off. His fellow workers emerged from the drain laughing. The troops I was with were visibly shaken by the cruelty of the incident as well as frustrated, because they had not been able to prevent it.

This is an example of how people think and act differently within their various cultures. Of course, Asiatics feel pain, fear death personally and know sorrow. Their culture, however, does not enable them to understand such feelings or to respect them in others.

Western culture has been influenced by Christian people whose faith has initiated more Christ-like ways of thinking about God, our neighbors, our country, the cosmos and ourselves. The Christian culture was surely transmitted by Christians with warm hearts and keen minds who did not hesitate to use and transform the language and cultural symbols of their lives. They spoke with the tongue of the Galileans, and the tongues of the Jews, Greeks and pagans.

Christ's witnesses in this world of the twentieth century have a comparable task: that of speaking in the tongues of both the marketplace and the university. The domination of today's culture by humanism may be a sad reflection on the intellectual sloth of people who have not bothered to think out, and through, our faith, nor given reasons for the hope that is in us.

I write this to remind Christians not to be afraid of thinking, researching, writing, painting, sculpting, dancing, healing, studying. We cannot jump out of our culture into a state of pure spiritual being unrelated to our bodies and minds. We either improve culture, or we denigrate it. All of us would be in a bad way today if Christians in the past had chosen to do the latter.

My position is, I think, similar to the one expressed by C.S. Lewis in his essay on "Christianity and Culture," which appears in his *Christian Reflections*. The points he makes are as follows:

1. As a Christian he was justified in earning his living as a teacher and critic of English literature. This was something he could do, and he did it well.

2. It was important that Christians like himself work among the "culture-sellers." They could at least be the evidence of the antidote to humanism.

3. Personally, he was grateful for his cultural activities, because they had given him "an enormous amount of pleasure." Pleasure in this sense is related to the joy of doing things well for the glory of God.

4. Culture provides a treasure-trove of "the best (sub-Christian) values." Although these values will save no one, they will enable a person to achieve a better understanding of his or her own faith. While an uneducated person may be apathetic and complacent, the cultured person cannot help but realize that reality is extremely odd. Whatever ultimate truth may be, it must surely have the characteristic of "strangeness." This is a point I appreciate greatly. The strangeness of Christianity was a factor in my conversion. It is, of course, bound to be different, because God and His Son, Jesus, are different from the state, humanism and secular culture. A recognition of such differences is often a prelude to discipleship. I confess that my faith has been strengthened by reading the works of thinkers who might be presumed to be hostile to Christianity.

Those who are committed to Jesus as Lord need have no fear of losing their faith because of their studies. One profound and devout thinker I respect has said he is grateful to everyone he has read and studied, for all of them have helped him to see Christ more clearly.

The believer, therefore, may find that his studies deepen and widen his Christian faith, and that he or she may contribute to the Christianizing of contemporary culture. All of us are in debt to those who have communicated their faith to us because of the intellectual disciplines they engaged in. Think of the excellence of the Gospels both in content and form; the profound faith and intellect of St. Paul, St. Augustine, Martin Luther, John Calvin, C.S. Lewis, Malcolm Muggeridge and thousands of others.

Education as a Synthesis

There are few in the academic world today who would claim that higher education provides salvation. A few decades ago the situation was different. Educators, politicians and commencement speakers spoke as though it did. The realities of existence, however, have decreed otherwise. The mood tends to be pessimistic. This, as I have written earlier, is a consequence of humanism's failure. A survey of the American university campus, published in 1977, bears this out. The survey was prepared by Semour Martin Lipset of Stanford University, and Everett Carll Ladd of the Social Science Data Centre, University of Connecticut.

This mood of pessimism was characterized as follows:

a. One in four faculty members admitted to having seriously considered, over the period of at least two years, the advisability of resigning.

b. One in three were exploring the possibility of work in non-academic fields.

c. Some of the reasons given for pessimism were:

1. Low salaries and slow promotion;

2. Decline of student interests and educational standards;

3. The loss of meaning and purpose by faculty and administration.

The positive side of this pessimism, however, is the growing awareness that the popular "*isms*" of campus life are now old and dying idols.

In an address at Princeton University, within the context of a prayer breakfast, on June 3, 1978, Dr. Jon Fuller, President, Great Lakes Colleges Association, had this to say: "Colleges and universities are enjoying reunions with their own spiritual heritage. Princeton was not unique in beginning in a parsonage. Many colleges began in much the same way. Recalling [this heritage] is helping institutions to come to know with their full educational potential—as places for the growth of the spirit, the body, the personality, as well as of the mind."

A similar flicker of light in the darkness came my way recently when I was lecturing at a college in the West. It is, I hope, a parable of, and for, our times. After my last lecture in a series, a man introduced himself as a professor of philosophy at a nearby state university. When he informed me of his position, I thought he would begin to tear apart my arguments, but that was not the case at all. He had come to learn from me. He went on to tell me his story.

He had been the victim of his own intellect, and his belief in logical positivism. So weary did he become in writing about it, teaching it, and existing by it, that he turned to hard liquor for refuge. His wife left him. His friends abandoned him. His university fired him. He was left with nothing but a bagful of words, a glass, a bottle and a dark, lonely saloon. He had dropped to the bottom. There, in his "pigsty," Alcoholics Anonymous picked him up, and introduced him to the saving grace of God in Jesus Christ. It was this grace that set him on his feet again. Now he is busy studying those philosophers who dared to relate their thinking to the reality of God's revelation. We talked for several hours while I shared with him the teaching of Christian thinkers whom I had found helpful.

But what has this to do with education as a synthesis? Simply this: human failure is invariably God's opportunity. The opportunity that humanism's pessimism evidences is that it is a faith that fails, that it cannot save, and that it leaves the campus open once again to think within the bright light of divine revelation.

Because of the integrating power of faith in Christ, the Christian may conceive of education as a means of synthesis. Our education, that is, does not begin with ourselves, our innate goodness or wisdom, our pet neuroses, the sociological predicates of the state, or popular consensus. It begins with God and the new mind He gives us for our new life in His kingdom. I am reminded of two sentences from an essay by C.S. Lewis: "When anyone comes into the presence of God, he will find, whether he wishes it or not, that all those things which seemed to make him so different from those of other times, or even from his earlier self, have fallen off him. He is back where he always was, where everyone always is."

I see this to mean that when we enter, by faith, into the freedom of God, we come to ourselves, as did the prodigal son when he left the far country for home. We are given the essential knowledge of ourselves that makes all other knowledge meaningful and significant. John Newton expressed it beautifully in the first stanza of his well-known hymn:

> Amazing grace! How sweet the sound—
> That saved a wretch like me!
> I once was lost but now am found,
> Was blind but now I see.

"*Now I see*," is the dynamic that makes for the authentic synthesis of all life and experience we call education. The best analysis of this is to be found in the ninth chapter of John's Gospel. The man, blind from birth, is given his sight by Jesus. Because He performed this healing miracle on a Sabbath, the religious people declared it could not be of God. Jesus was classified as a sinner. The once-blind man's reply to this criticism is remarkably sane: "Whether he be a sinner or no, I know not: one thing I know, that, whereas I was blind, now I see." He continued to see: first, that Jesus was a good man, for He could not have healed him unless God were with Him; second, that He must be at least a prophet; and third, that He was none other than the Son of God. This we may define as the ultimate vision that inspires our minds and illumines our brains.

In this light, Dr. John Hibben, Hegelian scholar, Presbyterian minister and university president, described the task of a university in 1925:

> Stevenson writes that the adventure of life is like a pilot starting out with his ship on a voyage to India, his only chart being that of the Thames and the port of London. On his long and dangerous voyage, all that he has to guide him is a local experience. So students of today have no adequate chart for the more adventurous voyage of life on which they are launching. In some way we must touch their imaginations. If I were asked what above all others would be my prayer for the young people of Princeton and of our country, I would reply: 'That they might have an enlightened imagination.' I feel they are missing sadly the great fact that there is a movement of the spirit across the history of mankind and that the great benefactors of mankind,

that have had a part in this movement of the spirit, are those who have contributed to the 'coming of the Kingdom of God upon the earth.' My wish and ambition is that our young people may not merely be looking on in the great happenings of this generation, but that they too may have a part in this eternal movement of the spirit.

This spirit of which he spoke, is nothing less than the power of grace which initiates all things, integrates all things and redeems all things. What better text is there for this than Colossians 1:13-18 in which St. Paul sums up the work of God in, and through, his dear Son:

Who hath delivered us from the power of darkness, and hath translated us into the kingdom of his dear Son: In whom we have redemption through his blood, even the forgiveness of sins: Who is the image of the invisible God, the firstborn of every creature: For by him were all things created, that are in heaven, and that are in earth, visible and invisible, whether they be thrones, or dominions, or principalities, or powers: all things were created by him, and for him: And he is before all things, and by him all things consist. And he is the head of the body, the church.

It is this vision and spirit that C.S. Lewis referred to when he wrote: "He is back where he always was, where everyone always is."

This vision brings all things together, and holds them together, in the synthesis that is truly educational. It integrates all that is true, relevant, useful, moral and meaningful.

One of the miracles that occurred when I was a prisoner of war of the Japanese in World War II was the creation of a jungle university. We had no board of trustees, no government grants, no library, no laboratories, no buildings. What we had was a community of faith that had come into being through the miracle of grace. Those prisoners who had been set free inwardly by grace wanted to know more of this grace. Their faith resulted in the desire to know more about God's world, God's work, God's people, God's ways and God's sons.

Our resources were former professors and lecturers who were with us, and those who asked them questions. Although the teachers had no notes, their students asked the right questions that evoked the right answers. I taught the New Testament, philosophy and introductory Greek. Probably the greatest miracle of all was revealed in a letter I received some years ago from a professor in Australia:

> I have just read your book, *Miracle on the River Kwai*, and learned from it that you are the teacher who introduced me to Greek and the New Testament. You succeeded in arousing my interest to the extent that I continued my education in the classics at a university here. For the past sixteen years, I have been teaching, and recently I have become head of the department. Thus, I am writing to express my gratitude for your inspiring instruction.

I wondered what my own teacher in my student days, Professor Dall, would have said to that. For I was no genius in that department.

That miracle of the jungle university was an expression of *the faith that seeks to know*, that sees God's glory in the heavens, the atoms, the amoeba and other human beings; and does so above all because it has seen that glory shining on the face of Jesus Christ, "full of grace and truth." It is He, as the integrating Word, who brings all knowledge and wisdom together in the synthesis of His truth.

What should we look for in a university?

First of all, realize there are basically three kinds of universities.

1. I shall begin with *the state university or community college.* We presume that these academic centers are secular in their orientation. Political pressures, particularly those initiated by minority groups, insist on interpreting the First Amendment as the separation of church and state, to mean that there is only one acceptable norm for education and that is secular humanism. Even where this principle is adhered to rigorously it cannot keep out the Christian faith: for it comes with people. At one very large and very secular state university, a friend of mine in the English department initiated a series of courses such as: *The Bible as Literature, The Early English Novelists and the Influence of the Bible, Religion and Its Influence on the Literature of the Renaissance.* She also began a prayer group. Thus, a Christian nucleus was formed as a center of Christian life, nurture and witness. There was no opposition. The Christians were free to be themselves.

I have been to at least a dozen state universities, at the invitation of their presidents or departments of philosophy, to lecture on Christian thought and to encourage a witness on campus. I mention this merely to indicate that as Christians in the world, we are not expected to be loved by the world, but to love the world. We are responsible for initiating the saving dialogue. A state university, as part of the world, is a glorious opportunity to support whatever witness is there. If there is none, then to initiate one. Where there is one

91

Christian, there are usually two. And when there are two or three, there is our Lord to witness through the two or three.

By using their intelligence, Christian students may help initiate courses relevant to the gospel, and encourage Christian faculty to bring their faith on to campus instead of leaving it behind in the local church Sunday by Sunday. Above all, remember this includes state universities.

2. *Private colleges that once were Christian.* There are many of these. Just as the ethos and character of state universities vary, so do those of private colleges. There are no stereotypes. What is true of one is seldom true of the other. Although secular humanism seems to dominate the private college campus, grace is not prevented from invading it. Usually this type of university prides itself on its academic excellence. Sometimes the pride is greater than the fact. It also boasts of its close faculty/student relationships. If this is the case, then it is a plus factor.

Briefly stated, here are some other positive factors offered by private colleges:

a. *The origin and history of the university or college.* Invariably it was founded by preachers, or concerned laymen, for the furthering of Christian thought and character amongst the young. Read the commencement addresses of the college presidents of the eighteenth and nineteenth centuries and usually you will find them calling their graduates to be exemplars of the Christian faith, good morals and vigorous piety.

At college convocations and other occasions, this Christian origin often slips out unexpectedly to the embarrassment of the humanists who had hoped that it had been buried once and for all. People of faith cast long shadows because they stand tall. Their influence is there to haunt the humanists and to challenge their unexamined premises.

b. The dormitories, dining halls, social facilities, debating clubs, choirs, glee clubs, museums, libraries and assembly halls indicate *the personal and communal quality of the university.* Usually there are monuments and memorials to remind everyone of its Christian origin, and also its Christian hope that all may be one in and through our Lord.

c. *The existence of a chapel* and its program of services, study groups and other events. I find that many young Christians fail to take advantage of the opportunities the chapel offers. They may do so because they fall for the lie of humanism that the worship of the living God is unimportant; or because they think it is not good enough for them. It is different from their hometown church and denomination. Its ecumenical nature is pridefully disdained. The failure of such chapels, when they fail, is invariably due to the failure of the campus Christians to stand up and be counted with the community of Christians.

d. *The existence of a chaplain* who is usually strong in his faith when he is supported, and usually weak when he is frequently criticized and rejected. The snobbishness of humanism very often seduces Christians into thinking they should only be Christians at home and not on campus. Thus, they fail to bear witness and inhibit others who are too timid to come out into the open. If you think the chaplain's faith is not up to your standard, go and speak to him about it. You may be surprised. You may even find your standard was not as high as you boasted it was.

3. *Christian colleges.* There are those which are Christian only in name, regulations and advertising

brochures.

There are those which are Christian in character, in faculty and in fact. My classification of an authentic Christian college is as follows:

a. It is Christian in atmosphere, or ethos, rather than in its rules recorded in its calendar or catalogue. What atmosphere would one expect to find other than love? This is what our Lord expects of us: "Love one another, as I have loved you" (John 15:12).

Never underestimate the power of this love: this is *agape*—love that seeks the well-being of the other. It is the means whereby truth is communicated and wisdom deepened. It is the atmosphere of freedom in which people grow to maturity. It is the open door to the community of Christians and to the kingdom of God. If we think we have no need of it, we are neither Christian nor human.

Once when I was teaching in the psychology department, I noticed that one of my students presented me with essays that were excellent in style and analysis, but weak in research. I called him in for a discussion. In the course of the interview I told him he had the intelligence to do better work. I asked him why he produced 'C' level results with the ability to achieve an 'A' average. In his reply, he told me he had come to the university from a high school where very few students went on to college. The consequence was that he felt himself to be inadequately prepared. So frightened was he of his new environment that he did poorly in his freshman year. He concluded that the best he could hope for was a 'C'; therefore, he pegged his intelligence at this level. Rather than doing his best, he got by with the minimum of concentration.

When he was leaving my study, he thanked me for my kindness in telling him he could do better. I was the first person who had ever told him that. How sad! This is a simple illustration, which I hope shows the practical and effective quality of the love St. Paul has written about so beautifully in 1 Corinthians 13.

I have had the privilege of visiting colleges where love was the active quality of their education. Students were helped by the compassion of their teachers to do better than they ever believed possible. A professor of mathematics once told me of a student who had been admitted with very low College Boards simply on the belief of the director of admissions that he was capable of enjoying the benefits of a higher education. It turned out that he enjoyed those benefits so well that he graduated Phi Beta Kappa and went on to gain a Ph.D. at a prestigious institution with a high rating in its physics and mathematics departments.

First John tells us that perfect love casts out fear. This is true at every level of existence, particularly the intellectual level. I find these days that the faith of humanism has inhibited so many young people that they are afraid of failing, afraid of not getting A's, afraid of not getting into medical school or law school, afraid of being moral, afraid of using the beneficial facilities of their university, afraid of being themselves and afraid of living. What a tragedy! The immobilization of fear is shown up for what it is by those who respond to the Teacher of Life. Remember how He commands us not to be anxious, but to come to Him so that we can learn from Him in the partnership of love.

We mature in love; for love is the atmosphere of life. Within this atmosphere we are better, and do better, than anywhere else. On the basis of this understanding, Albert Schweitzer wrote in his *Memoirs of Childhood and Youth*, "As a rule there are in everyone all sorts of good ideas, ready like tinder. But much of this tinder catches fire, or catches it successfully, only when it meets some flame or sparks from the outside, i.e., from some other person. Often, too, our own light goes out, and is rekindled by some experiences we go through with a fellow-man. Thus we have each of us cause to think with deep gratitude of those who have lighted the flames within us." As Christians we rejoice that our Lord has "lighted the flames within us," and because He has, no one may put them out. The Christian college, therefore, carries on the lively tradition initiated by Him.

When we think of a university's authority, we should think of it in those terms I have touched upon. This is the authority that grants it authenticity. One of the best criticisms I have heard of the humanist's position came from a young physicist I had known during his undergraduate and graduate days: "The university is insensitive to the cruelty of academic neutrality, which insists on giving no guidance to young people, and which refuses to accept any kind of responsibility for the disastrous consequences of such a policy. We do no one a favor by turning him loose on his own. What is this, but a cause of alienation?"

b. The dynamic of love transforms a Christian college into *a caring community*. Thus, its ambience is not that of the state, or the Educational Testing Service, but that of the church and the Christian family. With this understanding in earlier days, a university was described as *universitas magistrum et scholarium*, that is, a guild, or community, of masters and pupils living together in trust and love as they supported one another in the humble dedication to truth and the Lord of truth.

The humanists have never improved upon this model. It is so self-evident that they have been unable to reject it. Karl Jaspers, the German existentialist philosopher, for example, states, "All of university life depends upon the nature of the people participating in it. The character of a given university is determined by the professors appointed to it. . . . University life is no less dependent on students than on professors." He then goes on to point out that it is a privileged and special community, with a solidarity of interests, and a respect for excellence in every aspect of human existence. Without truth as its goal, it could not exist.

The basic model is, of course, the Church that began at Pentecost. This is the essential, life-giving community, the one to which the Christian college hopes to aspire. Its true existence is within the spiritual/personal dimension. This hope gives us a sense of *where* we are, because it is the visible evidence of *whose* we are. In this dimension we are given a sense of purpose, *eschaton* or end, and order. Without these, there is no personal, moral or intellectual integrity.

c. The third quality to look for in a Christian college is that of its *corporate morality*. This is the visible manifestation of its authority. It does not need to make a moral statement; *it is one*. Unlike a humanist institution, it exists to serve God, and do His will. Ultimate authority is not in people and their institutions, but in God, the supreme sovereign of the universe, and in His Son to whom He has given all authority and power. This is what we mean when we speak of Him as ascended to the right hand of God, the Father: in the position of executive power.

The truth by which we live is revealed, not manufactured by psychologists of education, or legislators in Congress. It is by this divine, eternal truth that all people, and their institutions, are judged. If we compare this with the position of the Humanist Manifesto II of 1973, we see the radical difference between the two faiths. So far as morals are concerned it declares: "Moral values derive their source from human experience. Ethics is autonomous and situational, needing no theological or ideological sanction. Ethics stems from human needs and interest. To deny this distorts the whole basis of life. Human life has meaning because we create and develop our futures. We strive for the good life, here and now." We have discussed the absurdity of this position in the earlier chapter dealing with the despair of humanism: a despair based upon that fact that individuals and nations become chaotic by denying the authority of God and doing what pleases themselves. I hope to touch upon the importance of Christian morality in a later chapter, but, for the present, it is necessary to reaffirm its biblical basis:

1. The Ten Commandments, as the irreducible minimum, stress our initial responsibility to God and our neighbors. The first four deal with our responsibility to God, and the second six deal with our responsibility to our neighbors based upon the imperative of the first four.

2. According to biblical thought, the uniqueness of being human is that we are aware of this responsibility and, as a consequence, know what is good. The prophet Micah has summed this up for us in his great passage: "He hath showed thee, O man, what is good; and what doth the Lord require of thee, but to do justly, and to love mercy, and to walk humbly with thy God?" (Mic. 6:8). This knowledge, Amos saw, was the divine plumb line by which Israel was both judged and redeemed.

3. The good required of us is seen plainly in the life, death and resurrection of Jesus, and in His teaching, particularly that which is contained in the Sermon on

the Mount (Matt. 5-7). Now we know what is good, and why it is so, and what is expected of us. We learn to be moral by being in the company of those who are moral. This characterizes the Christian college as the company of those who live their lives, as best they can, according to the example and teaching of Jesus. It is the moral people who create the moral ethos. That is why I wrote that a Christian college is known by its atmosphere. As Christians, we have a common mind. We know, that is, what it means to be a Christian, to think like one and to act like one. Jesus has shown what God would have us do.

The best illustration I can think of, regarding what this means, is drawn from my wartime experiences as a company commander in the 93rd Highlanders, an elite regiment in the British Army known as the Thin Red Line because it defeated the Russian heavy cavalry at the battle of Balaclava. In our action against the Japanese Army, we were often separated as companies from one another, and thus had to act independently. The directive of our commanding officer was, "I expect you to be in my mind, and do what you would expect me to do." Is not this what our Lord expects of us: to be in His mind? We know what His mind is. St. Paul tells us clearly in his letter to the young church in Philippi: "Let this mind be in you, which was also in Christ Jesus: Who, being in the form of God, thought it not robbery to be equal with God: But made himself of no reputation, and took upon him the form of a servant, and was made in the likeness of men: And being found in fashion as a man, he humbled himself, and became obedient unto death, even the death of the cross" (Phil. 2:5-8). This was Paul's way of telling the young Christians of Philippi how they were to compose themselves as the community of Christ in a secular city. His words have the same meaning as those of Jesus after He had laid aside His teacher's robe to wash His disciples' feet as a slave. "For I have given you an example, that ye should do as I have done to you" (John 14:15).

When one thinks of it, learning the mind of Christ is what the Christian life, and an authentic education, is all about. It takes more than four years, however. It takes a lifetime.

A word from experience.

In the hope that we learn from experience, it may be helpful to give a brief picture of my own involvement in a university over a period of twenty-five years. As a university, Princeton comes under the heading of my second category: Private colleges that once were Christian. Princeton is one of the fruits of the Great Awakening. During the first thirty years of its existence, 1746-1776, it became the first national college in the colonies; the college with the highest academic standards; and the college whose alumni contributed most to the moral, physical and spiritual well-being of the new country that grew out of the ashes of the old. Privilege, prosperity, fame and the popularity of humanism anesthetized its mind in the twentieth century.

I was called to be Dean of the University Chapel because the president at that time believed I could preach the gospel honestly, intelligently and relevantly. During the past twenty-five years, my freedom has never been challenged to preach the gospel, nor has my freedom to call out, preach to and instruct a community of Christians. The program of the University Chapel offers a rich fare of Bible study, theology, church history, ethics, prayer groups, conferences, retreats, daily services, as well as regular Sunday services at 11:00 A.M. The response to our witness varies. It may be classified broadly as follows:

a. Young Christians, who know they have much to learn, identify with the Chapel readily. They usually represent every shade of the denominational rainbow. These become the members of the visible community of Christians on campus who praise the Lord and love the brethren because they are turned to Jesus as their Lord, and revere Him as the center of life, and head of His body, the Church. They learn to be deacons, and serve one another as heads of committees and organizations. They also learn to teach the Bible, conduct services and counsel their peers. Usually by the time they graduate they are well educated as Christians as well as in their various academic disciplines.

b. Young Christians who believe they have nothing to learn. They usually do not like me because my accent is different—although it is the one God gave me. They do not like the University Chapel because it is too big and too much like a cathedral. They do not like those who do not think as they do. They worship off campus and hold their own meetings, which they classify as the only Christian ones. From time to time, they bring their own brand of speaker to their meetings. They believe they must separate themselves from the world, and from other Christians who know they have to live in it, but not by it.

c. Seekers who come to services and study groups in order to learn what the Christian faith is all about. These students usually become believers. They are welcomed and loved. As Cromwell once said: "To be a seeker is the next best thing to being a finder."

d. Those who classify themselves as agnostics and want to try out their humanist faith against the Christian faith. Most of them, if they are given time, freedom and love, become Christians. Many of them I find became agnostics in protest against some unhappy experience they had with Christians, usually of an authoritarian and legalistic nature.

e. Ex-humanists who presume they are not good enough to be associated with Christians because they have not been brought up in a Christian home and have not gone to Sunday school. We love them, and assure them God's grace is for all, especially them. After instruction, I baptize and confirm them, and they usually have a good track record. Sometimes those who start off far behind in the race who have to run with patience go on to lead the pack.

f. Troubled people. These are individuals who are troubled by fear, guilt and meaninglessness. Their minds are at the end of their tether. They have nowhere to go but death—by their own hands. They represent the end of humanism and its despair of existence. Their act of coming to see me, however, is evidence of grace. By grace they are found, and by grace they are saved. I am very glad to be there: for if I were not, there might be no one, as Christ's representative, to turn to.

I have come to realize I cannot save the campus on my own. Only God can do that. Those who are Christians may put themselves into His hands to allow Him to use them as He will. I am constantly surprised by grace. So often I have tried to do His will: prayed and studied hard, preached, taught and counseled; spent lots of time with students in anticipation of their making a personal commitment to God in Christ. And nothing seems to happen. Then, out of the blue, someone I have never heard of comes to tell me that something I did not think was important was the very thing that led him or her to a lively encounter with our living Lord. We may work for God once in a while, but He is working all the time. If we are faithful, we may do a little saving, but He alone gives the increase.

I thank God for the privilege of being at a university.

Last words

a. You do not have to go to university. You may choose to go just as you may choose not to go.

b. University is not to be feared. It is a means of helping you use the intellect God gave you. It provides the best means of answering your intellectual questions, the most interesting of which are likely to be those initiated by your faith in Jesus as Lord. So often asking the right question is more important than providing what you think is your own right answer.

c. Your time at university is to be used wisely. You have time to think for yourself: time to test your faith, your own faith, for while others may help and encourage there is no point in existing on a third-hand, and, usually, a third-rate, faith. There is time to be a better Christian, better prepared for the task God has in mind for you.

d. There is no such thing as a Christian in isolation unless it is in solitary confinement as a punishment for witnessing to the lordship of Jesus Christ. We are Christians in fellowship with God, through Jesus, and with His people. As I have said earlier, where there is one Christian, there are usually two or three. Join them. If there is a university chapel, belong to it. You will learn much from those who have different backgrounds from yourself. You went, or you are going, to university to learn, are you not?

What might you expect to note as the identifying marks of the Church? Here are three guides; the first is ancient, the second is reformed, and the third is my own, drawn from experience, and added to the first two. The Church is:

One

a. *One*, because there is one Lord and one baptism and one God, the Father above all.

b. *Holy*, because the Church is Christ's creation, brought into being by the power of the Holy Spirit, and baptized with the blood of the saints and martyrs.

c. *Catholic*, because it is Christ's Church in the world confessing the one Lord Jesus and His rule of faith and discipline, and continuing in the faith of the apostles.

d. *Apostolic*, because our faith today is the same kind and quality as the apostles'. We believe in the same Lord Jesus, in the same Father, and in the same Holy Spirit. There is one apostolic succession and it is that of the one faith initiated by God, in Jesus, through the Holy Spirit, and lived in every generation by those our Lord has called, and who have responded.

Two

a. Where the Word is *rightly preached*.

b. Where the sacraments are *rightly administered*.

c. Where the discipline of Christ's love is *rightly maintained*.

Three

a. *Ecumenical*, because it is Christ's Church, in the world for which He died, recognizing no national, racial, sexual or economic barriers: for in Christ we are all one.

b. *Evangelical:* this is what the Church is all about, to witness by word and action to the total claim of the total gospel upon the total individual and the total world.

c. *Existential:* do not be frightened by this one. It merely means according to our own personal experience. By the work of the Holy Spirit, we experience individually sin, repentance, conversion, the freedom of grace, the new life as the new person in the fellowship of the Holy Spirit. Our individual experiences are valid. In terms of our faith, they are our own original response to God's grace. They matter. They are not, however, an end in themselves. They are the consequence of the Holy Spirit's action, and, therefore, point away from themselves to Him.

The thing to do is to use your faith like an anchor. Let it go, and go up and down with the waves. Or, to change the metaphor, the more you use it, the stronger it grows. The more you hedge it in with fearsome precautions, the more it is likely to die. Faith, after all, is a risky business. Look what it did to Jesus! Trust God. Trust your fellow Christians. Live your faith. Love your neighbor.

The prayer of the happy Christians at college is something like this:

Father, grant us day by day the joy of living in your presence. Your love overcomes our fears. Help us to live bravely, think bravely, and act bravely for you today. There are so many who need you, but don't know it. May we become your means of grace to them; through Jesus Christ our Lord.

The more you understand the nature of your own faith, and the nature of the university, the more you will improve both of them. It is a privilege to be a member of a university as a student. It is also a privilege to bear witness to your Lord.

6

The Challenge of the Christian Faith to the University

Too often Christians presume that humanists are secure in their own faith. They are not. There are a few exceptions perhaps, but only a few. The humanists' faith can always be challenged more effectively than can our Christian one. For the most part, they are concerned about reality. And what is more real than the substance of the Bible and the gospel, both of which are centered upon God's revelation of himself in Jesus Christ. In an interview with Malcolm Muggeridge, which appeared in the April 21, 1978, issue of *Christianity Today*, Mr. Muggeridge testified that the only reality he found in a world of confusion and fantasy was the reality of the Christian faith.

Malcolm Muggeridge, you may recall, is a literary intellectual who found humanism to be saturated with illusions. It was with a great deal of relief that he turned to the Christian faith, shortly after the death of a beloved son. It is this reality, of which he speaks, that is the constant challenge to the university. I have tried to point out that our faith as Christians is not "our own thing." On the contrary, it is our response to the reality of God who has revealed himself. The object of our faith, therefore, is not the sum total of human thought, or philosophical propositions.

As we mature in our faith, and in knowledge, we

become better prepared to challenge intelligently the false idols of humanism. If Christians do not provide the challenge, who will? What I have found is that where Christians have failed, because of intellectual sloth or prideful indifference, all kinds of charlatans have moved in to claim the soul of the campus. The contemporary campus is the prime marketplace for peddlers of fake wares such as TM, est, Zen, the Moonies, The Way, and a variety of gnostic cults dressed up to look like new and better forms of Christianity.

There are many reasons why the purveyors of instant bliss do so well. One is the failure of Christians to be Christians, and the other is the insecurity of university people in general. Humanism is the idol that fails. Its failures are evidenced everywhere. Aldous Huxley wrote his novel, *Brave New World,* as its epitaph. This novel is an accurate portrayal of contemporary humanism's existence, although it was written after a visit to the city of New York in 1928/29. A fellow intellectual wrote to him, accusing him of being a traitor to the cause of humanism. In his reply Huxley challenged the criticism in these words: *si monumentum requiris circumspice,* which means: "if you seek evidence, look around you."

The evidence is plentiful. Malcolm Muggeridge speaks ironically of it:

> One of the many pleasures of old age is to become ever more sharply aware of the many mercies and blessings God showers upon us. Almost every day I discover new ones. What joy, for instance, to be confronted with power and authority in disarray in all their guises everywhere! How reassuring and diverting to find all our egotistic pursuits

being made to seem devisory! As the quest for money, by the presses that print more and more of it, and the Arab sheiks into whose artless hands more and more of it falls. As carnality, by erotomania and porn, the *reductio ad absurdum* of sex, and accompanying sterility rites and inexorable drift into impotence. As celebrity, by the media which bestows it so lavishly on auto-cued news readers, cinematic beauty queens, miming pop stars and grunting prize-fighters. As knowledge, by sociology and kindred studies, with their computers, public opinion polls and other devices for making false deductions from incorrect data. I could go on and on: if C.S. Lewis were alive today, he would, I feel sure, have Screwtape complaining to his lord and master, Old Nick himself, that there was scarcely one plausible vice left on the calendar.

People in universities are looking around to see the evidence. They do not like what they see. Humanism has failed. Who will challenge it?

As Christians it is a time to count our blessings. There are many to support our challenge. Not so long ago, there were those who presumed, along with Descartes, that reality could be reduced to a mathematical formula. Now physicists and mathematicians are telling us there is no such formula. In a recent article, Professor John Wheeler, the distinguished astrophysicist, pointed out that there are no systems of numbers available for the task. It would take something akin to magical numbers to begin with. What he sees of the world is just one vast mystery. His role in the face of this mystery, he maintains, is that of discovering how things operate in the world of physics. His knowledge of physics, however, does not explain the mystery. On the contrary; it increases it.

In a similar vein, Professor John Turkevitch, a physical chemist, once told me: "Fifty years ago scientists in my field believed that within fifty years they would discover ultimate matter. And do you know where ultimate matter is now? Away out there somewhere, and going away from us so fast that we can never catch up with it!"

The enormous increase of knowledge has not solved the vast mystery. It has only enlarged it. Knowledge has been like a balloon: the more you blow it up, the greater is the surface confronting the mystery. In this light, the English philosopher, C.E.M. Joad, wrote of his conversion in these words: "If it is not wishful thinking, if it is not the dictate of an arbitrary will to believe that has brought me to Christianity, I see no alternative to the conclusion that the main impulsion is from the intellect. It is because the religious view of the universe seems to me to cover more of the facts of experience than any other that I have been gradually led to embrace it" *(The Recovery of Belief)*.

This confession is a low-keyed one which expresses the humiliation of intellectual pride. The intellect has nowhere to go without the guidance of the Christian faith. This faith, however, is not something you import into the intellectual scene by the yard or the pound. It has to grow within it. Thus, the need for Christian intellectuals to reap the fields that are "white unto harvest" is very great.

Due to the fact that many Christians have been intellectually lazy in expressing the mind of Christ, and morally lazy in their failure to challenge the premises of humanism, other faiths have rushed in to fill the vacuum, as I have mentioned earlier. It is important to face these expressions. See them for what they are. Do not be overcome by their threats. Evaluate them in the light of Christian wisdom.

Humanism's Alternatives to Humanism

The first of these is *mysticism*. Usually what is described as mysticism is likely to be centered on one's inner feelings, and the means of achieving them. During the 1960s Timothy Leary, a professor of psychology at Harvard, advocated the religion of LSD, which he described as the League of Spiritual Development. By means of this psychedelic drug, LSD, the individual's consciousness was supposedly enlarged. The experience induced was to be the same as that experienced as conversion at mass evangelical rallies. The presumption of some, if not of Dr. Leary, was that LSD, and similar consciousness-changing drugs, had replaced religion and God.

This cult gave no evidence of clear thinking, compassion for the oppressed or moral responsibility. The basic concern was for the self and its experience of the "trip" or "high."

The emphasis of this cult is upon individual ecstasy for its own sake, that is, the ecstasy of the *ego* by means of the *ego*. What does this add up to, but the continuous reinforcement of selfishness. Ecstasy soon becomes depression. And "a way out trip" becomes a trip to a mental institution.

I have been interested in the claims of Transcendental Meditation practitioners to overcome the power of gravitation by elevation. That is, floating the body in the atmosphere without any visible signs of support. What is this but the attempt to claim individual divinity? (Compare this with our Lord's second temptation.) My skepticism of this cult is based upon my knowledge of the *ego's* great ability to deceive itself.

111

Once in Bombay I watched a *guru* place a mango seed on the ground. He made incantations over it and then described the transformation of the seed into a mango tree. He told his audience that he was climbing the tree, that he was descending from the tree and that the tree would now disappear.

An Indian guide, who was with me, clapped enthusiastically with the rest, turned to me to say, "Wasn't that marvelous?"

"Marvelous?" I exclaimed. "What was marvelous?"

"What he did, of course!"

"I did not see a thing." He received my reply with astonishment. So far as he was concerned, everything that the *guru* had said had happened. After shaking his head in despair over my disbelief, he suddenly pointed to the mango seed.

"There," he shouted excitedly, "there is the evidence. The mango tree was turned into a seed."

I said nothing. There was little point in telling him the mango seed had been there from the beginning and had never been more than a mango seed.

Much of what is classified as mysticism is simply a self-induced illusion. As such, it is again evidence of humanism's failure, and of the need for individuals to make some kind of meaning out of the ashes of their despair.

I need not enlarge upon this theme. The evidence is everywhere: in the worship of the stars and the messages of one's horoscope; in fortunetelling; spiritualism; magic—black and white; Satanism; self-hypnosis; and wishful thinking.

Hinduism and Buddhism
The mood of mysticism seems to have encouraged interest in other expressions, such as Oriental religions,

particularly Hinduism and Buddhism.

Hinduism is so wide in its range that you can choose whatever aspect of it that suits you. It ranges from a high mysticism and asceticism to a low pornography. The most extreme expression, I think, was the cult of the *Thugs* who worshiped the female destroyer of men, *Kali*. She is depicted with men's skulls hanging from her belt. The Thugs were robbers who murdered their victims in a prescribed ceremonial way, and in the same way were expert at breaking their victims' bones so that they could be buried in the smallest possible grave.

Hinduism has sometimes been described as the highest form of spirituality by its Western advocates. The best reply to this statement may be found in Albert Schweitzer's *World Religions* or Arthur Koestler's *The Lotus and the Robot.*

I have lived with Indians, watched them practice their religion and studied it. I am grateful for my experience because it helped me to see that personal salvation, and human worth, lay in a different direction.

In Hinduism, there is no real world. There is only *maya*, illusion. And there is no real existence; it is *karma*, fatalistic determinism. This sense of participation in illusion pervades every form of thought and relationship. And why not? The world is not real, and neither are you, so why bother about anything? Prepare for the moment of enlightenment, by preparing for death. The best one can hope for is a total absorption into the cosmic consciousness, and salvation in the void. The worst that may happen is reincarnation into a lower caste group.

I once heard a professor, who had never been east of Chicago, say that Hinduism offered the only religious alternative for Western intellectuals. This is a daft statement, but one, alas, which some people take seriously.

Buddhism is a reformation movement within Brahman Hinduism initiated by Siddhartha Gautama. Buddha is the title given to him, signifying "the *enlightened* one." He tried the acceptable Hindu ways of meditation, charity and asceticism. He found no enlightenment through them. He concluded that the real problem is existence itself, which creates its own misery. Existence is a vicious circle. It is characterized by desire; desire results in birth; birth results in suffering; suffering results in death; death results in reincarnation. Desire binds us to this world that is not real; therefore, if we were to abandon desire, we would be bound no longer by the endless chain of reincarnations. We would cease to exist—to be. We would be at rest in the indifference of *nirvana*, where there is neither change nor conflict. And this is a contradiction in terms: what *is* ultimately is nothingness. Thus *nirvana*, in Christian terms, is the second death. The ultimate bliss is to be dead forever. This is as far as mysticism can take us.

For those who seek non-involvement and non-commitment, the Hindu-Buddhist way is attractive. It is not to me. Perhaps for very good and practical reasons. On the Kwai Noi River, I was in a prison camp that was commanded by a devout Zen Buddhist colonel. So devout was he that he was reluctant to be involved in the deaths of those he had condemned. Whenever he put on his monk's robe and departed for his meditation, we knew we were in trouble. We would be given no food for a week, assigned impossible work tasks, and half a dozen of our colleagues would be executed. After the unpleasant business of punishment was carried out by his subordinates, he would return smiling. I cannot help but feel there is a moral in my sad tale for today.

You will find inevitably that campus conversations will include free and plentiful discussions on the greatness of mysticism and instant Zen (i.e., Zen minus its Japanese disciplines). If you want to be popular, you can learn the groovy terms in a few minutes. If you are a Christian, however, and mention your Lord's name in reverence, you will become unpopular very quickly. To speak of Him is regarded as anathema. Why? Because it marks you as being intolerant, non-intellectual and superstitious. Those who will mark you freely as such will, of course, have learned their toleration from their morning horoscope and the *guru* of the moment.

Our critics may mock us, but we have no right to mock them. We may listen, smile, make our witness and leave the rest to the Holy Spirit. I do not think young Christians make a good witness by being against everything in a self-righteous way. True tolerance is to know what you believe, to be confident in your faith and to be tolerant of others for Christ's sake. It is He who loves the other through us. Through His eyes, we see everyone as the brother or sister for whom He died.

So far as other religions are concerned, we do not spend our time condemning them. We can do much better by being obedient to Jesus and His words. C.S. Lewis has written, "If you are a Christian, you are free to think that all these religions, even the queerest ones, contain at least some hint of the truth." Having said that, he goes on to write, "As in arithmetic, there is only one right answer to a sum." The right answer is also the right way at the right time, which is God's time.

Christian Mysticism

Now I have to say something good about mysticism. What is required is that we discern between a true and a false mystical experience. The former, William James tells us, will lead us to the heavens, while the latter will lead us to the pit. Discern between non-Christian and Christian mysticism. The former is focused upon ourselves, the latter upon Jesus, our Lord.

The goal of Christian mysticism is to know the presence of God through the man Jesus. What we, as Christians, may speak of as mystical is to be aware that we are in the divine presence. In the presence of the one who says most tenderly, most compassionately, "Behold, I stand at the door, and knock: if any man hear my voice, and open the door, I will come in to him, and will sup with him, and he with me" (Rev. 3:20). The best commentary on this text is George Herbert's *Love Bade Me Welcome*. St. Paul tells us that we "Walk not after the flesh, but after the Spirit. . . to be spiritually minded is life and peace" (Rom. 8:4-6). Paul also reminds us that although we walk after the spirit, we do so in the flesh. The flesh is not debased, but glorified, for "it is the temple of the Holy Spirit." I take this to mean that our existence is real, in a real world. In this real situation, however, God comes to us. Not the other way around. That is why I keep writing of the Christian faith as our response to God's initiative. What do we do when someone taps us on the shoulder, but turn to see who is there? And who is there? The man on the cross!

It is the reality of God who is there that makes all the difference. Read 2 Corinthians 12 once again, and recall how St. Paul puts the mystical experience in its proper place by glorying in his infirmities. Through

116

them, he had heard his Lord say, "My strength is sufficient for thee: for my strength is made perfect in weakness" (2 Cor. 12:9). Remember, too, that it is as a saved man, one who has been born again in the Spirit, that he writes, "For I know that in me. . .dwelleth no good thing: for to will is present with me; but how to perform that which is good I find not. For the good that I would I do not: but the evil which I would not, that I do" (Rom. 7:18, 19). Thus we learn from Christians such as St. Paul that we are not to seek the mystical experience for its sake alone, neither are we to try and be the super-man or super-woman who claims to be more spiritual than other Christians. To be faithful to the mystical vision means, first of all, being faithful to our Lord who is with us, and secondly, faithful to our sisters and brothers. In the words of St. Paul, "Let all things be done unto edifying" (1 Cor. 14:26).

Do not be afraid of the mystical experience. When it happens, glorify God in the name of Christ. The spiritual life is real. What do we mean by spiritual? Is it not simply the inner life we call the soul or spirit? It is metaphysical: more than physical; metasocial: more than society; metareligious: more than religious propositions or manifestations. Only within our spirits may we experience the Holy Spirit. Not by reason alone, and certainly not by blind obedience to religious precepts.

When we read of the literary prophets, we read of those who heard God speak in their spirits so clearly that they said, "Thus saith the Lord." And did not David dance before the Lord (2 Sam. 6:14-16)? The Church after all was not organized by a decree from Caesar, nor by the instructions of a council of bishops, nor by the blueprints of theologians, but by the Holy Spirit. Without the inner life of the Spirit, there is no

Church. She, as Christ's bride, lives by the Spirit, and by those gifts of the Spirit that we designate as charismatic. We do not, however, boast of these gifts, knowing that the greatest gift of all is to say, "Jesus is the Lord" (1 Cor. 12:3). And to say this in the Spirit is to do what He commands.

In my twenty-five years of university ministry, I have found that no intellectual has been influenced by mass evangelism, or by theological brilliance. What I have found is that some have been so influenced by Christians who lived their faith in obedience that they, too, have committed themselves to their Lord. The Christian faith is still a possibility for many humanist intellectuals in a way that rational dogmatism never is.

Even the most died-in-the-wool humanist is a human being who knows loneliness, guilt, weakness and personal failure. He or she may also admit, in moments of honesty, that there may be someone greater than the physical universe who ought to be worshiped. Where reason has failed, the presence of Christ has not, and it takes someone to assure another that Christ is with us. I agree with Dietrich Bonhoeffer who said, "The Christ in my heart is weak. The Christ in the heart of my brother is strong. Therefore, I need my brother."

This means: do not judge your fellow intellectuals, senior or junior, for not being Christian. Leave the judgment to God, and introduce them to Jesus as your Lord. In recognizing this truth, we are able to see that it is only Jesus who can heal the inward and spiritual sickness of the intellecutal.

The Christian Challenge to the Bureaucracy of Humanism

The interest in mysticism on campuses is often a

romantic rebellion against the impersonalism of mass society, and massive bureaucracy. We have seen how humanists have affirmed *man* only by denying him. For Marx, *man* meant the classless society. For rationalists, *man* meant the rational process. For naturalists, *man* meant a fortuitous combination of chemicals. For the behaviorists, *man* means the master plan of behavioral engineers. For the university administrator, *man* means the product of education. For university trustees, *man* means money, bricks and cement. Humanism has thus created a monster who is loose in the world to destroy its manufacturers. Humanists would like to escape from the clutches of this destructive monster. But how are they to know how unless a Christian tells them? In a later chapter, I shall deal more fully with God's view of man. At the moment, it is sufficient to remind you that the Christian faith is the only one in the world which exalts every woman, man and child in every generation and country.

The bureaucracy of humanism's making cannot think in terms of people and individuals, but only in terms of the faceless mass, the sacred intellectual formula, and the verification of the computer. So far as individuals are concerned, they do not exist. Feodor Dostoevski (1821-81), Nikolai Berdyaev (1874-1948), Martin Buber (1878-1965) and Aleksandr Solzhenitsyn (1918-) have written about this most compellingly.

a. Dostoevski's Legend of the Grand Inquisitor, in *The Brothers Karamazov*, tells the story of Jesus' return to Seville. As he walks alone, and sadly, in the crowd, the Grand Inquisitor spots him and throws him into prison. In the death cell, he tells Jesus why he has to die again. Why? Because Jesus trusted individuals too much. By doing so, He granted them too much freedom. He, the Grand Inquisitor, is the humanist who sees that this freedom is a burden too heavy for anyone to bear; therefore, he has eased this burden by abolishing individual freedom and giving the masses what they want. What is this? Bread, and all that bread implies, including power, privilege, oppression, slavery and war. Thus, the Grand Inquisitor is repeating the temptations already presented to Jesus in the wilderness by Satan.

It is the age-old story. Grand inquisitors, tyrants, kings, dictators, behavioral engineers, master planners, sociological and economic experts have chosen to take the place of Jesus Christ for the sake of people's physical well-being. They offer materialistic security in exchange for one's soul.

The answer of our Lord remains the same: "Man shall not live by bread alone, but by every word that proceedeth out of the mouth of God" (Matt. 4:4). This answer is more applicable today than ever. Another Russian, Vladimir Solveov, who lived about the same time as Dostoevski, wrote an essay about the world's unification for peace under the directorship of the world's top humanist. The only obstacle, however, to world unity is the three branches of the Christian Church: the Orthodox, the Roman Catholic and the Reformed. These communions refuse to worship anyone as Lord, but Jesus. The humanist declares war on them. In response, the Church unites and is organically one at last. United by faith in Christ, the Church stands alone in the last battle of all: that of Armageddon, the battle that is now being waged, although in its early stages.

b. Berdyaev was a Russian intellectual Marxist who was influenced by Dostoevski. He traced the Communist movement to its roots in Western humanism. He saw the consequences of this all around him, in the denigration of human beings and the affirmation of absolute power on the part of state bureaucracies. In his testimony, he tells of how it was freedom that brought him to Christ. He became an apostle of freedom. In 1921 he was sacked from his position as professor of philosophy at Moscow University, and was, fortunately, able to leave Russia that year along with a number of other Christian intellectuals. Most of his exile was spent in Paris, where he died, in the suburb of Clamart in 1948. He was a prolific writer whose theme was constant: our freedom is in Christ, the only free man, who is truly free because He is truly man and truly God. Departments of philosophy, under the influence of logical-positivism, have disregarded his testimony and philosophy.

c. Martin Buber is a Jewish philosopher well known for his *I and Thou.* He reacted against the sterility of nineteenth-century humanism by creating a biblically based personalist philosophy. In this philosophy, he pointed to the uniqueness of human beings who cannot be thought of as things, but only as conscious beings, who are conscious of each other through their consciousness of the divine I AM. He provides a language and thought style which are helpful tools in the communication of Christian thought. His analysis of contemporary civilization is similar to that of the others I have mentioned. In one memorable passage from *Between Man and Man,* he defines our modern predicament as a struggle between the humanists of the left and those of the right. Those of the left, who wish to abolish memory, and those of the right, who wish to control it, march together in the mass—into oblivion.

d. By this time Aleksandr Solzhenitsyn is a

household name. When he criticized Russian Communism by showing us that Russia was one vast prison camp in which people are dehumanized, he was very popular in this country. Recently, however, the press has become disenchanted with him because of speeches similar to the one he gave at the Harvard Commencement of 1978. The reason is that he has placed the United States, and the West generally, in the same category as the Russian State. Although his position may be regarded as extreme, we may say, nevertheless, that it is a true one. In essence it is similar to my criticism of our civilization, which has abandoned the Christian faith and lost its soul in exchange for garbage.

These four men I have mentioned are only four among many who have shown us why, and how, Christians are duty bound by their faith to challenge humanism's domain, particularly on the campus where it originates.

Very simply we may point out that once we lose faith in God we lose faith in each other. We no longer live in a relationship of trust, but under the thralldom of bureaucratic laws. The missing factor in humanism's formula is human freedom. Turning once again to Dostoevski, we may trace at least three, or perhaps four, forms of freedom:

a. Even in a perfectly planned, perfectly organized and perfectly controlled society, there are those who choose to be free, even absurdly free. *The Underground Man* of Dostoevski's story introduces us to the individual who refuses to be "a stop in the organ." For unknown and purely intuitive reasons, he stands up to shout his defiance at the bureaucrats. What is this "underground man" but that quality of the soul, within each of us, which is expressed at unforeseen moments in acts of rebellion and defiance. The story of student life over the past six hundred years gives plenty of examples of this form of freedom.

It was in plentiful evidence during the decade of the sixties. I trace this rebellion to the University of California at Berkeley in the mid-sixties. The president of the university had been widely acclaimed as a great educator for introducing the concept of the multi-university. I took this to mean a conglomeration of educational conditioning units operating with the maximum of rationalist efficiency and the minimum of human concern. In effect it was similar to the picture I have drawn earlier of the university conceived as a technological processing plant. Each student is processed for admission, processed for courses, and processed for graduation. He or she is placed on a production belt to be delivered as a finished product with a B.A., B.Sc., M.A. or Ph.D. stamped on the bottom, and conditioned to take one's place in a similar processing plant whether it be for the manufacture of bombs or of citizens.

The first phase of the Berkeley revolt was simply a rebellion of "the underground man" against the technological process. It was quickly taken over, however, by organized Marxist groups such as the Students for a Democratic Society. Then followed the second phase which was characterized by posters, slogans, crude four-letter words and violence. Thus, the quality of basic freedom is replaced by a less rational, and more destructive form of humanism. Of this Dostoevski has also written in his prophetic novel, *The Possessed.*

b. The irrational quality of freedom expressed in "the underground man" is also evidenced in the man of the flesh who acts both irrationally and irresponsibly.

He in turn is easily controlled by the one who evidences the third quality of freedom:

c. That of making two plus two equal four. This is the freedom to be rational which results in humanism, and in its own contradiction. The rational person who uses this freedom to turn against God and walk away from Him becomes the tyrant or murderer, no matter how unwillingly.

d. The ultimate experience of freedom is that of turning to God to accept His forgiveness and love. Dostoevski illustrates this in his novel, *The Idiot*, which is a story of a prince who lays aside his earthly position and power to be a fool for Christ's sake. Critics, I fear, often miss this point and thus claim it to be Dostoevski's poorest work. Perhaps the best portrayal of authentic spiritual freedom is to be seen in Aloysha, the third of the brothers Karamazov. He is the one who fulfills his freedom in the spirit through Christ and learns to love everyone, even in his sins, to love everything in the whole of creation. By doing so, he begins to learn of the divine mystery behind all things.

By understanding the nature of freedom, we are in a better position to challenge the campus cries of academic and selfish freedom. The true story of our freedom is told in the Bible. The preface to the giving of the Ten Commandments is the divine statement to the Jewish people: "I am the Lord your God who brought you out of the land of Egypt, out of the house of bondage" (Exod. 20:2 RSV). When Jesus preached His first sermon in Nazareth after His temptations, He read from the scroll of Isaiah at the sixty-first chapter, and proclaimed that this prophecy was now being fulfilled by Him. He is the liberator who sets free the bruised and broken victims of existence from their death cells. It was on this basis that St. Paul wrote to the foolish Galatians, telling them to stand fast in the freedom for which Christ set them free.

I have written of this theme of freedom for the very good reason that there can be no individuals of worth without it. Here again we are referred to the ultimacy of our spiritual freedom which is centered in Christ. When we are liberated by Him, we are free indeed. Freedom begins in the spirit, and is active in Christ's community of love. We are learning we cannot live by bread alone, but by every word that God speaks. And what is the ultimate Word? Jesus has told us: "I am the bread of life" (John 6:35). We live through Him, and by Him, and in Him.

The validity of this truth may be tested by the reaction to it, even in the simplest of terms. For example, in 1977, President Carter laid down as a primary premise of foreign policy the principle of human rights. The Iranian government attacked it on the basis that the United States should respect those nations "where certain political niceties are sacrificed, and certain libertarian corners are cut, in order to ensure maximum economic growth." The Soviet position was similar. It claimed the right to subordinate individual human rights for the sake of strengthening the socialist system which alone has eliminated unemployment, discrimination and hooliganism. And so continues the argument of the Grand Inquisitor: take bread and forget about spiritual freedom.

The Moral Challenge

Just as the community of Christians is free to challenge the impersonalism and tyranny of bureaucratic tyranny, so is it free to challenge the moral character, or lack of it, of the university in which it

exists. Usually university administration will point
out that morality is not part of the university's
business. Why? Because morality is a personal matter.
It is up to each individual to adopt, and live by, the
values of his or her choosing. The only business of a
university is the advancement, and communication, of
knowledge. In this way, knowledge is reduced to
materialistic data verifiable by scientific methods
alone. What is this but a symptom of tunnel vision?
And, of course, it is not true that morality has no place
in the intellectual society.

Secular morality is no morality at all. Hobbes has
already pointed out for our benefit that if every
individual is free to seek his own happiness, he will
disregard that of others and contribute only to that
which pleases him. He will do "his own thing,"
regardless of the consequences to others.

This point was made most clearly on a program I
heard broadcast by a college radio station. A popular
singer from England was being interviewed. At one
point he was asked what he thought of contemporary
ethics.

"Jolly good," he replied. "Anything goes. What I
mean is we are free to do what we like. No holds
barred. You don't want to hurt anyone, of course, not
unless you have to."

The interviewer asked him to expand this thought.

"It's like this, see. I believe in being kind to Granny. I
don't mean her no harm, that is. But if there came a
time when she got in my way, I'd have to kick her in the
teeth, see. That goes for everything else as well, the
Government, the Church—yes, I'd say particularly the
Church. It's always moping about what you can't do.
It's silly. No harm in a pint, a bit o' grass, or a bit of the
you-know-what with a girl, or a bit of whatever you

fancy. I draw the line at murder, mind you. Can't get away with that too often, can you?"

Most old-fashioned campus humanists would be shocked by such a statement. C.S. Lewis has pointed out in his *Men Without Chests* that educators deny morality within their institutions yet are astonished when young people take them at their word and demonstrate their lack of it. Thus, the virtue of the young Englishman's statement was that it was honest. This is what he had heard, in more abstract prose, of course, this is what he had seen, and this is what he had come to believe.

Educators usually defend themselves by saying that this is not what they mean. Of course, there must be morality. But the university *qua* university cannot adopt and support a core of values. That must be left to each individual. Where he or she learns these values is purely a personal and subjective matter. I hear this *apologia* for amorality almost weekly, and it is nonsense.

Without a remnant of what is essentially Christian morality, universities would not exist in their present form. Their goodness, like the goodness of a bad apple, is that of being a university. An example of a university that lost its goodness is that of the Free University of Berlin. It was founded after World War II with the blessings of American intellectuals and U.S. government money. The "Free" meant freedom from traditional morality and thought. On the Marxian premise that all in the past is bad, this institution set out to live by the standards of the future. It has ended up as a non-university.

A similar situation was depicted in one of the episodes of a British TV series entitled, "The Glittering Prizes." In a new, swinging college, dedicated to the sociological way, undergraduates who tried to be conventional were "flunked out"; V.D. was no worse than a common cold; copulation was in the same category as brushing your teeth; and compassion for another was a symptom of sociological weakness.

Let me illustrate the absurdity of the amoral position by referring to an incident involving one of my Christian friends in a department of urban studies. He was being considered for promotion from associate to full professor. The promotion process included a number of statements by undergraduates about their experience in his courses. He was confident of promotion. His confidence was shattered when the committee informed him he did not meet their standards. He appealed, but the committee turned his appeal down by saying that his case was closed, and could not be reopened. With the support of a few professors, who testified to the excellence of his academic work, he appealed to the president. The president ordered an investigation which allowed my friend to read through his file. He discovered that the undergraduates who had testified against him, all of them women, had never taken any of his courses. He visited them individually. All of them admitted they had presented false evidence. After considerable probing, they further admitted that they had done so because professor so and so threatened to fail them if they did not conform with his instructions. Using the same form of blackmail, he was having sexual intercourse with all of them.

This incident speaks for itself. So far as my own experiences of contemporary philosophy are concerned, I see little hope of returning to a moral philosophy which takes Christian values seriously. It is obvious that "the acids of modernity" have eaten through the ethical structures of philosophy. One group of thinkers tells us that morality is not a matter of what one ought to do, but of what people do in general every day of their lives. To make a moral statement one must, first of all, take a popular poll. If 51 percent say that they cheat on their income tax returns, then this is moral. Or if 51 percent or more say that they commit adultery, then adultery is moral. Another group will lose you in a verbal maze. It will distinguish between substantive ethics, normative ethics, meta-ethics, situational ethics and so on in such a way that few students know what morality is all about except that it is simply a matter of verbal definition. For example, one might talk about a metaphysical statement as one which is about a normative statement, but is not itself a normative statement, except when normative statements about normative statements are indeed normative statements. Once you get the hang of it, you may have great fun in the same way that you have in playing a game of contract bridge. To keep the game going, you may go on to speak of utilitarianism, ideal utilitarianism, intuitionism, naturalism, emotive-ism, criteria-ism, modificationism, all of which suggest we have come a long way from the common sense school introduced to this country by John Witherspoon, and still further from the Sermon on the Mount.

I do not know how a typically "modern" moral philosopher would respond to a student who was naive enough to go to him and confess, "I have sinned." Most probably he would question the statement by showing there is no such thing as a sin, for it cannot be seen as a sin because there is no way of measuring whether or not it could be a sin, and then suggesting a visit to the campus counseling service where words such as sin were not allowed to happen.

The same moral confusion reigning in society reigns on the campus. When we designate it as amoral, that is lacking in a sense of right or wrong, good or evil, we are merely using a euphemism for immoral. In Christian terms, the greatest immorality is that of being unaware of immorality.

No matter how costly it may be in terms of popularity, Christians cannot sit back and say, "None of my business." It is; or else if it is not, you are in the same position as the humanist: the utmost immorality is no morality.

Again, the evidence on the campus scene is that we cannot ignore the moral problem. On many campuses there are student groups, such as Students for a Holistic Education, Hunger Action Committee, Society for Racial Equality in South Africa and so on. They are raising the moral question, but where do they go for answers? They are providing us with the opportunity of saying something for our Lord's sake.

Christian Morality

What is Christian morality but the visible evidence of our faith? God calls us to be His kinsmen, His holy kids, if you wish to use a contemporary expression. This means a new relationship, one evidenced by love—the *agape* or divine love. And is not this love the ultimate form of morality? St. Paul tells us of this: "For in Jesus Christ neither circumcision availeth any thing, nor uncircumcision; *but faith which worketh by love*"(Gal. 5:6 italics mine). The translation of the New English Bible makes this abundantly clear, "faith active in love." St. John tells us the same thing both in John 15, and in 1 John 4:11-21. This latter portion begins, "Beloved, if God so loved us, we ought also to love one another," and ends, "And this commandment have we from him, That he who loveth God love his brother also." Before I enlarge upon the ethics of *agape,* perhaps we ought to take a quick glance at the biblical picture.

As human beings we are created to be moral. We are given a sense of what is right and wrong. It is possible to argue that this means different things to different people in different times and places. It may. But only to a limited extent. Despite minor differences, we know what is good when we see it. The pagan, Roman centurion observed Jesus for three hours on the cross, and concluded, "Truly this was the Son of God" (Matt. 27:54). Observe, by the way, that Caiaphas saw the same man over a longer period of time. Despite his training in the Torah, and in the Temple cult, the best he ever said of Jesus was, "It is expedient for us that one man should die for the people, and that the whole nation perish not" (John 11:50). Perhaps the reason the centurion saw what the priest did not was that the priest had lost his vision. It is of this vision that the wise man writes when he says, "Where there is no vision, the people perish"; another version of this is, "Where there is no moral authority, the people run amok" (Prov. 29:18).

The prophets took it for granted that there was an inner vision enabling people to recognize the good. "He hath shewed thee, O man, what is good; and what doth the Lord require of thee, but to do justly, and to love mercy, and to walk humbly with thy God?" (Mic. 6:8). This, like the Decalogue we have discussed earlier, is the basic requirement. This is the least God requires of us—of all of us, Christian and humanist alike. St. Paul affirms this, particularly in the first two chapters of his letter to the Romans. In these passages, he tells us that as our faith increases, so does our consciousness of

God's righteousness—the righteousness not of law but of grace. When faith decreases so does our moral sense. And note this: "For the wrath of God is revealed from heaven against all ungodliness and unrighteousness of men, who hold the truth in unrighteousness; Because that which may be known of God is manifest in them; *for God hath shewed it unto them*"(Rom. 1:18, 19 italics mine). Thus, the sin is not that of ignorance, but that of not doing what is known to be right. Is not this the paradox of the university? It knows, but what it knows, it does not. The humanists have chosen not to obey the moral predicates that God has revealed to them inwardly. "Therefore thou art inexcusable, O man, whosoever thou art that judgest: for wherein thou judgest another; thou condemnest thyself; for thou that judgest doest the same things" (Rom. 2:1).

If God expects the minimum of everyone, He also expects the maximum. The Sermon on the Mount is to be taken seriously. It has sometimes been called "the impossible ethics" because it is 180 degrees different from what is commonly referred to as morality. That it is different from secular ethics is made clear deliberately by the way it begins.

1. Jesus goes up into a mountain and takes His seat. This means He affirmed His authority. It is similar to speaking of the university as a *seat* of learning, or to the academic authority of Professor Blank of the chair of the humanities. Having placed Jesus in the seat of ultimate authority, St. Matthew tells us that, "He opened his mouth, and taught them saying" (Matt. 5:2).

2. What He said was radically different from the acceptable norm of His time, and our time. How popular are the Beatitudes even among Christians?

a. Blessed are the humiliated—those who are

landless, lawless, powerless. The kingdom of heaven is theirs, because they possess it with empty hands and a full heart.

b. Blessed are those who weep, who are saddened by the cruelty and evil of this world. They shall become strong by faith.

c. Blessed are those disciplined by suffering, because of their poverty. The earth is theirs to possess by love.

d. Blessed are those who hunger for the divine righteousness, rather than the righteousness of this world. They shall be satisfied.

e. Blessed are those who do mercy, for they shall receive it.

f. Blessed are those who are true to the inward vision, and who are single of purpose: for they shall behold the King in all His glory.

g. Blessed are those who glory in war, and in the manufacturing of armaments? Not a chance! Blessed are the peacemakers! They are the children of God. (As an old soldier, this troubles me—in the moral sense. There is no means of avoiding the challenge. It is a tough one!)

h. Blessed are those who are successful and work in the White House; and all the newspapers speak well of them?

Here we have the irreducible minimum of the Christian life—the life lived by faith in Jesus. What an interesting university we could build on this ethical foundation.

In the rest of His Sermon, our Lord shows us it is what is inside that counts. *What we believe, we do!* On this basis, Jesus also said: "I am the vine, ye are the branches: He that abideth in me, and I in him, the same bringeth forth much fruit: for without me ye can do nothing" (John 15:5). By faith, that center of inwardness, we allow Jesus to reign within us. Where

He reigns, His presence is visible. An illustration of this truth comes from Africa. A missionary retraced the steps of David Livingstone some thirty years after his death. He stopped at a village and told the villagers of Jesus. After he had finished, one old lady said to him, "I've seen Jesus. He came here thirty years ago to visit us."

A less pleasant story comes out of my own experience in prison camp. One of the men instrumental in showing me Jesus, and saving my life, was Dusty Miller. He was a saint. The glory of his Lord shone through his flesh. Toward the end of the war he was chosen for the task of cutting a retreat route through the jungle for the defeated Japanese Army in Burma. The officer in command believed his emperor was divine. His troops, therefore, could not be defeated. But they were. Therefore, they were being defeated by a power greater than that of the emperor. He thought he saw this power active in Dusty. To overcome it, he had him crucified. He was nailed to a tree. Because he was dying too slowly for his liking, the officer slashed him with his *samurai* sword. He was disemboweled. In the utmost agony, he died as a witness to his Lord.

Yes, Jesus is Lord of our spirits. The spiritual and the inner life are the same thing. There are new glimmerings of this on the campus which help to reinforce our challenge. One of these is the neurologists' realization that the brain and the spirit are not the same. One of the greatest neurologists, Wilder Penfield, concluded, after a lifetime of research and brain surgery, that a dualism cannot be denied. In his last book, *The Mystery of the Mind*, he says that at one time he presumed the mind could be assumed to be the upper stem of the brain. His study, however, led him to see that whatever the mind is, it is not the brain. The brain is like a computer, but the mind is like energy, or soul, or spirit.

As a Christian, I presume that the mind or spirit has the ability of responding to the moral imperative of the divine will. In Jesus we see what it is like for the human and the divine wills to be one. What Jesus believed, He did. The Sermon on the Mount was not only preached by Him, but lived by Him.

No one, not even the most tunnel-minded scientist, can escape from the moral challenge. We do not create our own morality. It exists before we conceive it. Having written this, I must go on to say that the newness of the Sermon on the Mount is the newness of Jesus who fulfilled the moral demand of His Father. He was not only perfectly obedient, He was perfectly faithful. Faith was completed and brought to its ultimate expression in His life of perfect love. He is the Word, the Principle, the Standard, the Norm of all morality in every age and place and civilization and university. Because He is, He spoke of himself as the I AM, the Amen of God, the Truth, the Way, the Life, the Light of the World, the Bread of Heaven. He is the Word who was in the beginning with God, who is the Alpha and Omega, the Creator, Savior and Judge of the world. He alone is worthy "to open the book, and to loose the seven seals thereof" (Rev. 5:2).

Amos, in the seventh chapter, shows us a picture of God standing upon a wall built by the plumb line He holds in His hand. The question He asks Amos is: "What seest thou?" And of course what he sees is the plumb line. This is the standard for Israel, the standard by which it was to live. In the same way, Jesus is the plumb line for everyone. There is no other standard that is more exalted.

Victor Gallantz was a publisher in England who

was famous for his Left Wing Book Club. He was brought up as a Jew, and I presume he was an active socialist, in theory at least. I heard him speak of his life in an interview broadcast by the Third Programme of the BBC. He answered a question about his faith by saying he was not religious in a conventional sense. Religion for him meant living the moral life, the good life, the life for others. The ultimate expression of this life he found in Jesus. He towers so high above all of us that He alone could be designated God. As one brought up in the Jewish religion to believe that one could not forgive the enemies of the Jews, he found Jesus' teaching on forgiveness to be beautifully sublime. He referred to the following passage: "Ye have heard that it hath been said, An eye for an eye, and a tooth for a tooth: But I say unto you, That ye resist not evil: but whosoever shall smite thee on thy right cheek, turn to him the other also. . . . But I say unto you, Love your enemies, bless them that curse you, do good to them that hate you, and pray for them which despitefully use you, and persecute you; That ye may be the children of your Father" (Matt. 5:38-45). And remember, it was this same man who said, "Father forgive them; for they know not what they do" (Luke 23:34). He did what He taught.

When we speak, therefore, of the moral challenge to the university, we are speaking of the challenge of Jesus. His challenge on the campus is mediated through those who obey Him. If you like, you could think of Him as the moral governor of the universe; this is truly what He is. It is He who brings order to our disorder, and saves us from the destruction of chaos.

I think of His role in the following way:

a. When we turn to Him as Lord and allow Him to reign within us by faith, we find that He integrates our lives emotionally, intellectually and morally. He makes us whole. Like a garbage man, He picks up the junk of our disordered lives, and gets rid of it, thereby tidying us up inwardly. We are subject, that is, to the harmonizing influence of His will. We become whole people. This is the same as being holy.

b. Having tidied us up inwardly, He enables us to conform to the form, or norm, of His eternal moral decree, the ultimate nature of which is love. This love is the moral order active among people. Have not you found this to be the case? I have! Wherever His love reigns there is peace, order, tranquility, joy among people. These are the characteristics of Christ's Church as the fellowship of the Holy Spirit.

c. Christ's rule of love, active in His community, contributes to the moral order of the neighborhood in which we live with our neighbors. This in turn contributes to the meaning, and purpose of life for everyone. This is why campuses borrow heavily from the riches of Christian credit without recognizing their debt to Jesus, who is also Lord of the campus.

As I see it, my task on campus is to claim it for Christ. How may I do this?

By prayer.

By worship.

By fellowship.

By witness.

By testimony.

By action.

By thought.

But above all:

By love.

Campuses today have many brilliant people, many scientifically capable intellectuals, but too few good people. I take exception to the prevailing view that goodness and intellect need not exist together. I think they do! This is what is meant by the Greek word for *excellence*, a word so often abused by commencement speakers. Both go together. I am convinced that an amoral, immoral intellectual is not only a bad person, but, in the end, a bad thinker. He or she is more akin to the devil than a drunkard or a whore. If you do not believe me, read the description of Satan in the first chapter of Job. He is the top intellectual, the head examiner, the rational judge.

The Challenge of Worship and Witness

In the previous chapter, I referred to the importance of the worshiping community of Christians. I did so because young Christians often rate it at the bottom of their interests. The top interests usually have to do with evangelical campaigns, conferences and spiritual retreats. What happens after they have been held? Very little, so far as I have been able to ascertain. The same people go to them. The same people return. And of those who return, the numbers decrease. Have these events by all means. But make sure there is something to return to! Yes, Christian fellowship! But what is the primary purpose of a Christian fellowship? Is it not to glorify God, and to enjoy Him forever? According to the Shorter Catechism, this is our chief end, or purpose. In a similar vein, St. Paul writes: "I beseech you therefore, brethren, by the mercies of God, that ye present your bodies a living sacrifice, holy, acceptable unto God, which is your reasonable service" (Rom. 12:1).

The habit of going off to the denominational church of your choice is a poor witness. It conforms to the ethical mood of the campus: *Do your own thing.* The best witness I can think of is the witness of the worshiping

fellowship on campus. Here are my reasons:
  a. The best witness to the campus is by those who are Christians in the campus.
  b. The higher the degree of visibility of professors, administrators, graduate and undergraduate students, and alumni/alumnae, the clearer and stronger the witness. For one thing, it marks each Christian as a member of a communion that has existed for nearly two thousand years. And for another, it is a public declaration that you esteem the company of fellow Christians higher than that of your peers.
  c. By worship, Christians are giving Christ His worth, and thereby declaring that He is Lord of the intellect, Lord of the will, Lord of the heart, Lord of our actions, Lord of the campus and nation, Lord of all. Lord, here and now. Never underestimate the power of praise. Once, in prison camp, I was leading a service of worship at dawn. I was seized by two guards, and beaten up. I returned to the service after the beating. I was beaten up on the spot. I continued again with black eyes and bleeding lips. This time the guards let me continue. They did so, I think, because it dawned on them that I was not doing my own thing. Along with my brothers, I was doing my "reasonable service." The only thing that could have stopped me at that time was death.

Albert Einstein is reported to have said that during the years of Hitler's dominance, he had hoped that the German universities would have opposed him. To his regret, they did not. To his delight the confessing Church did. Most of its members, by the way, were less fortunate than I. Their last act of worship was martyrdom.

If there is a college or university chapel, join it! Do not stand back and say it is not good enough for you! Remember, the Lord saw fit to lay aside His glory to become a man, as a man to be a slave, and as a slave to die on a slave's cross! Lay aside your mantle of self-righteousness and take the risk of getting your feet wet. If you do not, you are not free to witness. That is right: you are not free! Not free to transcend the limiting barriers of your pride. Not free to share your gifts of the spirit with others. Not free to be the humblest member of Christ's body. Not free to stand up and be counted with the least of Christ's brethren. Where Jesus is worshiped as Lord, do you have the temerity to say He is not the Lord of your choice? Of course you do not, as a Christian!

If there is no chapel, but there is a worshiping fellowship, join it regardless of the denominational tag, or lack of it.

If there is no such fellowship, initiate one. Find the two or three other Christians. Post a notice on the bulletin board to say that you worship at room B of Founders' Hall, at 11:00 A.M. on Sundays. Bring your faith, your guitar and your pipe organ—if you have one. Seek out a Christian professor, or janitor, or administrator. There are usually one or two or three hanging around, waiting to be asked.

Witness by worship. As you do so, you will find it renews your strength so you will become strong enough to witness in the lecture hall, the lab, the gym, the dining hall, the dorm, the student center, the extra-extra-curricular activity.

You may be tempted to witness only to a select few Christians who recognize only those who cross the proper denominational "t's" or dot the correct doctrinal "i's" as they themselves do. Overcome it! Take a risk on

Jesus who said, "If any man will do his will, he shall know of the doctrine, whether it be of God, or whether I speak of myself" (John 7:17), and "Search the scriptures; for in them ye think ye have eternal life: and they are they which testify to me" (John 5:39).

To be obedient to Jesus as Lord means that your faith becomes observable. Others see who you are because they know whose you are. The best commentary on witness I know of is the tenth chapter of Romans. Here, St. Paul reminds us that we are guided by the righteousness of faith, which is the righteousness of grace. Being in this righteousness keeps us in Christ's presence. He is with us in the mouth and in the heart; and in the heart and in the mouth. St. Paul uses a Rabbinic parallelism to illustrate the integrity of faith and action, action and faith. What we believe in our hearts, we say with our lips; what we say with our lips, we do with our lives, and *vice versa*. The earth is indeed the Lord's. As his kinsmen and ambassadors, we are privileged to bear the evidence of his lordship in every place where we are, and to whom we are with. Our vocation is to be His disciples. You need never worry about opportunities. There are more than you can possibly imagine. All we have to do is to let them happen. What is expected of us is faithfulness. When we are attentive, God creates the opportunity. Take, for example, the story of Philip and the Ethiopian eunuch. While he was being driven from the Temple in his chariot, he was reading the fifty-third chapter of Isaiah. Philip was standing by the roadside. He recognized that this was God's moment, jumped into the chariot, explained the meaning of the passage and baptized the Ethiopian at his request.

The word that comes through us comes in God's

time, and in His way. The miracle is that it comes. When a professor or student is faithful day by day, the word is heard and seen. If not today, then tomorrow. While writing this chapter, my personal challenge was challenged. It was in this way: an alumnus magazine published an interview with me about Princeton's Christian tradition. I had pointed out that the Christian presidents of the past had cast long shadows because they were men of big faith. They had left us a lively tradition of which many were still aware.

I also declared that it was my belief that some students had turned to Jesus as Lord, and that it was my hope many more would do so in the very near future. In saying this, I was merely saying what many presidents of the University had said in the past. At the time of the interview I was particularly interested in the letter of a former president, James McCosh, accepting the appointment offered him in 1868. At that time, he was Professor of Moral Philosophy at Queen's College in Belfast. He states the reason for his acceptance as follows:

> My past experience as a minister, first in the Church of Scotland, and latterly as a Professor in an Established University in these Kingdoms inclined me to believe that with God's Blessing my wide studies may be turned to some use. I feel especially that I might have more freedom there to promote the cause of Christ than in a state college in this divided country that is Ireland.

To promote "the cause of Christ" was the purpose for which I was called to Princeton. Often I have prayed to be more faithful to this call. Never less! An alumnus, however, suggested I should be less faithful. He sent me the following letter in the summer of 1978.

Dear Dr. Gordon:

The Spring issue of *Prospect* contained reports of an interview with you that may or may not accurately reflect your views but which does reflect, I believe, an underlying thrust which leaves me a bit uneasy.

I refer to my understanding of your position that it is only through Christianity that young people may gain the spiritual and moral direction they need and that indeed, "Western Civilization is nothing without the initiative and dynamic of Jesus."

Certainly as Dean of the University Chapel you have the right to speak as a Christian, and I share with you not only an awe of the greatness of this tradition but also the belief that the University has an important obligation to "relate values to our students."

What then is my concern? Certainly religious libertarianism is a universal issue involving all faiths, but because Jewish students would clearly constitute the largest religious minority at Princeton and because Christians and Jews bear a special relationship, one to the other, let me deal solely with these two groups.

Few paradoxes are sharper or more disturbing than that a people who have given so much to others have been in turn the recipients of so much suffering, part of which as been at the hands of the Christian community.

Since the earliest of times, the unfortunate contribution of Christianity to anti-semitism has been a well-established fact. The denial of the

143

great resources of the Jewish faith, unwillingness to accept Judaism as a valid path, within itself, to salvation, and dangerously biased texts have all helped to create an atmosphere that has been, and still remains, unhealthy for both Christians and Jews.

We simply have ignored the fact that nowhere in the teaching of the Synoptic Jesus does one have to become a Christian to be saved. We simply have ignored the admonition to accept the affirmations of wise men as to their beliefs when such affirmations are based on their own experiences but to reject or ignore their denials of what others may find rewarding as such denials are most often bred in ignorance.

All of the above may be somewhat of an over-reaction to the *Prospect* article. But my sense of your comments leads me to feel that non-Christians on campus may indeed not believe that the University's religious leadership is, in reality, openly facing them in a relationship of mutual respect.

We have much to learn from Judaism, as well as other religions, and it seems to me that Christians will best be served, and serve others, not by affirming superiority but through open acceptance of others as they are.

I considered this letter seriously, prayed about it, and sent the following reply.

Your letter has reached me at my summer retreat where I am trying to write a manuscript which I hope will be published. The subject may interest you. It is basically a critique of humanism in the light of Christian thought.

I am not sure I can answer your letter to your satisfaction. For one thing, an adequate answer would be too long, and for another, I am not sure what your question is. As I interpret it, you are:

a. Uneasy about my views reported in the *Prospect* interview. My views, as I remember, were those of a man trying to be honest. I was asked what I thought about it. Could I have said that it was not Christian? That would have been a lie. Should I have said that the tradition as Christian did not matter? That too would have been a lie.

b. Uneasy in case my views threaten the religious freedom of students, particularly those who are within the framework of the Jewish faith. The reason for your uneasiness is the history of persecution suffered by the Jewish people, particularly at the hands of "the Christian community." I agree that the history of this persecution is a long one dating from the eighth century B.C. up to our present time in the reign of the Nazis and the Communists. I disagree, however, with your all-embracing premise, "the Christian community." This means all Christians in every place and time. I presume you do not mean this. Yes, some Christian institutions at some times and in some places have persecuted some Jews. I lament this fact. I also lament the persecution of non-Jews. I trace the history of "the Christian persecution" back to 380 A.D. And not to Jews but to heretical Christians. I refer to the execution of Bishop Priscilla by the civil powers of Rome with the consent of the Bishop of Rome. This marks two things:

1. The unholy alliance of the *Roman* Church and the Roman State in the fourth century A.D. In a matter of three hundred years the persecuted community of Christians in that secular city was elevated to a position of eminence in which it lived in tension. I deplore this unholy alliance with its eventual resolution passing into the hands of the secular power. By the eleventh/twelfth centuries the Holy Roman Emperor claimed the power of death over heretics. Ancestors of mine were executed by this power for being of the community of Christians known as Reformed or Protestant. By the fourth century the church in Rome was only one of many. Did those other communities persecute Jews, or anyone else for that matter? I know of many instances of such communities being slaughtered by pagan Rome and other secular powers for the offense of being Christian.

2. I deplore the history of the Roman church and its persecutions. I also appreciate its contribution to the development of Western civilization, the vitality of which may be measured by the development of the citizens' awareness of their unique individuality. This awareness was surely the cause of the Reformation and the Renaissance. I was nurtured in a Reformed society, ordained in a Reformed Church, and know of no instance of persecution of Jews in the past four hun-

dred years. Both the people and the books of the Old Testament were revered; so much so that the Mosaic laws were absorbed into civil law, and divinity students, such as myself, had to be proficient in Hebrew before being admitted to the colleges of divinity. At examination time many felt that they were the victims of persecution.

Out of such a matrix the country of 1776 A.D. was born. Three of those who signed the Declaration of Independence were graduates of my own little Scottish *alma mater*. And out of the Great Awakening was born the College of New Jersey in 1746 A.D.

Experience and the facts of history keep getting in my way so you must excuse my reference to them. I refer to them, however, simply to express my concern about your concern. If not every community of Christians has honored Jews and their tradition, many have, just as many Christians have given their lives for Jews at times of persecution. But now to your third point:

c. I take it that you believe the expression and articulation of the Christian faith implies the unwillingness to recognize "the great resources of the Jewish faith, etc." You do not present any evidence for this serious charge so I do not know what you have in mind. I was of the opinion that I am well informed on the Jewish faith, at least well enough to conduct Jewish services and to counsel Jewish students in the absence of a rabbi. As a Christian, I I appropriate the Jewish tradition as essential for my faith and its understanding. I take it as a basic facet of the Christian faith that "all

147

Israel shall be saved" (Rom. 11:26) and that a true Jew is one who is so in heart. The rabbis I have known on campus have expressed the hope that the University Chapel be truly Christian in its witness, and not merely a dressed up version of American humanism. Their reason for saying this is that such a witness reinforces rather than weakens the Jewish one. If I were to say that being a Christian is of no real importance, I would also be saying the same about being a Jew. Jewish and Christian teachers know what unites and divides them. The four main differences are:

1. What the Torah is to the Jew, Jesus is to the Christian.
2. The Jew believes that the Messiah has not come—some even believe He will not come— while the Christian believes He has come in Jesus whose kingdom is not of this world.
3. Jews believe that no Jew may forgive another for a sin against a fellow Jew; Christians affirm that they cannot come to God unless they have forgiven all who have sinned against them.
4. The Christian witness has emphasized that God is the God of, and for, all people, and that the Covenant made with Abraham is one open to all who choose to enter into it.
d. Yes, of course, Jesus does not say that everyone has to be a Christian, but He does expect those who are attentive to Him to follow Him and obey Him. You will have read the Sermon on the Mount and its conclusion. I regret to say that I do not know the meaning of your third from the last paragraph. At a wild

guess I might answer that both the faith of a Jew and the faith of a Christian are initiated by the external, or objective, revelation of God.

Your penultimate paragraph could be conceived as being in bad taste. I do not choose to conceive of it in this way. The test of my leadership, for this is what you challenge, is best tested by non-Christians who are free to be non-Christians. To recognize them as such does not imply a denial of "a relationship of mutual respect." Would I gain that respect if I were to speak as a humanist, which I was once, but which I am no longer? Could I be trusted as a thinker if I did not confess my bias as a Christian?

No one, least of all myself, has tried to deny the substance of your last sentence. To be honest, I have to say that if I did not follow Jesus, I would not be particularly interested in other people or their faiths. And I certainly would not be at Princeton.

In the U.S.S.R., Christian and Jews are free to believe, but not to witness. I presume you would affirm our constitutional right to believe, and to witness.

I am glad you enjoyed four productive years at Princeton and that you hold no brief against it for its humble, if Christian, origin. I am sorry you could not have had me as a teacher or adviser.

I presume upon your goodness by enclosing a copy of my "Golden Jubilee" sermon. If you would like to have a watching brief on my witness, do not hesitate to complete, and send in, the coupon on the last page.

Do visit me in Princeton.

I send you my blessing.

As you see, I tried to be as explicit and as practical as I could in the hope that my letter might be used to initiate a stir in his intellect and his conscience. What the outcome will be I do not know. I leave that to the Holy Spirit.

I have referred to this incident merely to show that once you are involved in witness, you will be given the opportunity for more witness. Much of this witnessing requires patience, hard work and compassion. If we are not there on the campus, who will there be to make the witness?

To conclude this chapter, I shall emphasize again that the challenger to the campus is our Lord. He challenges every aspect of human existence and awareness because He is the center of relationships. I see this truth illustrated by the following diagram:

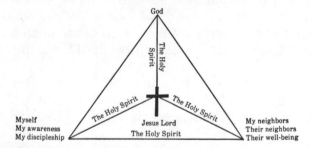

Through Jesus, the Lord, I am challenged to be my true self, both bad and good. I am challenged, in loving Jesus, to love God as Abba, Dad, or Father. I am also challenged to love my neighbors in this neighborhood. If I am a student, then my neighborhood is mainly the campus, and my neighbors, my colleagues. In this complexity of relationship, the Holy Spirit, as the bond of love between the Father and the Son, and the Son and the Father, is ever active. His activity is love by which we love God through Jesus, and through Him we love our neighbors.

7

What Is the Measure of a Man or a Woman?

When you go to a university that has lost its soul and its intellect to humanism, you will hear all kinds of people talking glibly about solving the problems of the world by studying man. This is the sort of thing that Alexander Pope said in his eighteenth-century work, *Essay on Man.* There is an appealing ring about such a simplistic belief. If man is the measure of all things, then how easy it is to use this rule—or so it seems until you try applying it. Once we start looking for the infallible measure, we find that it is nowhere to be found. Analyze a woman or a man anatomically, chemically, physiologically, biologically, psychologically, neurologically, or sexually and you will find there is too much to measure in one sense, and too little in another. To find anything approaching a universal norm is questionable. Once you get through dissecting a man or a woman, there is little left that is recognizably human. All there is is the same substance that you see displayed in a butcher's shop, anatomy lab, chemist's shelf or in *Playboy.* Man as the norm is not far removed from the one used by the ancient Roman soothsayers, namely that of disemboweling a hen or cock in order to foretell events by chucking the entrails on the ground.

It is reasonably intellectual to ask, "What is this man

that is the measure?" Do not be surprised, however, if your question is answered by a blank stare, or a startled gasp. Both of which are meant to imply that:

a. Everyone knows, so why be so stupid as to ask such a meaningless question?

b. Don't ask me that. I've never thought about it, and I'm not sure I want to begin now.

Eventually, after four or more years of advanced study, you may work out the answers that have been implicit in your courses, as being essentially four, plus or minus a few frills, trills and variations.

1. The first, and perhaps noblest, is that of a man or a woman as *a rational being*. You may, of course, find a few true believers left to deny the faculty of reason to those of the female sex, but they are becoming rare, and should be preserved for posterity wherever possible.

As you have concluded rightly, the norm here is not a man or a woman, but *reason*. You will have heard that the Greeks of old regarded it as a good thing. By means of reason, a man—seldom a woman—could mount the ladder of contemplation all the way to the top. There at the top, all the splendid wares of the ultimate good were displayed, such as forms, concepts, ideas, the real, and all of them unsullied by the dusty finger marks of existence. Reason was also believed to be a substance so fine that it was a force, or *logos*, or fire, or breath, or spirit. This reason is an activity which holds everything together in tension in the way that cement bonds a wall. The Stoics, of whom you have heard, were remarkably reasonable in their belief in reason, or perhaps I should write optimistic instead of reasonable, for they equated reason with human nature. Thus, if you followed your human nature, everything would be all right in the end. It was bound to be. It was the divine spark. To be good meant that you allowed reason to rule your life. All you had to be was rational—something that anyone could be as it was natural.

I have the impression that to be natural, or rational, also meant being aloof, cold, passionless. Indeed, Stoic *gurus* urged their students not to be involved too intimately with others. Kiss your wife if you have to, but do not love her. Reason is above love, and the reasonable man is too reasonable to be too concerned about anyone else.

The English idea of a gentleman was modeled on this pattern. He is the man of the golden mean who disdains passion, avoids the commitment required by faith, and upholds an existence that is moderately good. It is not surprising, therefore, to learn that English thinkers were the first to believe in the religion of reason in modern times. Such a religion involved the reasonable man in a search for those principles of Christianity which could be universalized, and therefore accepted by all reasonable men. Human reason was thus in the position of framing a set of doctrines which could be tested by reason alone without reference to the revealed truth of the Bible. Voltaire, for example, defined natural religion as those principles of morality that are held in common by all people. And Immanuel Kant declared in his *Critique of Pure Reason* that there are only three arguments for God's existence. The first is the argument from design, the second is the argument from a first cause, and the third is the ontological argument. These arguments, he claimed, are evident to speculative reason.

Many departments of religion still uphold this religion of reason as the justification for their presence on the campus, and regard the study of religion in the same light that a sociologist will study society. Any kind of religious involvement, such as prayer or worship, is looked upon as a threat to their rational objectivity.

In the end, the belief in man as *the bearer of reason* can take us no further than a computer factory where logical machines are programmed to calculate the conclusions of problems that are already determined by their unexamined premises. Although reason has been found to be fallible, this view still holds its own court in most campuses. The bloody wars of the twentieth century, the holocausts, the rise of dictatorships and the stupidities of bureaucracies have, apparently, been outside the tunnel vision of those believers in reason who believe that belief is irrational.

2. *Man, the happy, or unhappy accident.* You might be astonished that people who hold such a view would bother to go to a university. Next time you bump into a believer of this kind, ask him. He will probably become very angry and curse you for your impudence. But do not be upset; you might start him thinking. Human existence, as accidental, is the logical conclusion to the belief that God did not create the universe, or the first man. A combination of chemicals brought the cosmos into being, and another fortuitous, or nonfortuitous, combination of chemicals brought human beings into existence. They have kept themselves in being by eating, and drinking and procreating. These three functions are the only arguments for our existence. So far as any unique worth is concerned, this is to be regarded as an unhappy illusion due to the

malfunctioning of the chemical process. What may distinguish us from the rest of creation is that we wear clothes, and when properly trained, can operate computers.

Do not avoid forming a friendship with a believer of this type. His capacity for faith is so great that a little be-ye-kind-to-one-another-caring is likely to direct his faith to someone worthy of it. Many a potential saint is buried under the debris of skepticism, anxiety, gloom and despair that such people use to cover themselves. And who can blame them? If you are only an accident, you can be no better than an unhappy one. The cruelest accident of all would be your awareness that this is all you are, or are ever likely to be. The portrait of such a miserable believer is surely that of Sartre's *Nausea*.

3. *The social product.* Those who believe the universe is the consequence of the evolutionary process, or matter in motion, have sufficient faith to believe it is society which produces man as a man, and thus elevates him from his lowly animal ancestry. The proper study of man is thus no longer man, but society. Our study will, therefore, deal with natural and artificial environments, climate, natural resources, food, sexual habits, family, group selection, cultural forms, communication, economic institutions and social data of every kind.

I am not suggesting that you should not study sociology. You should. If you do, do not expect to receive the answer to the problem of human existence. You may find help in identifying the problem as well as increasing your awareness of its immensity.

Once we believe in human beings as social products, we end up by doing the following:

We give absolute worth to the state. This was well

exemplified by Hegel's view. He believed that the absolute idea had reached its synthesis in the emergence of the Prussian state. The highest service a subject could perform was to give his life in defense of his country. We can see how this belief dominated so much of nineteenth-century thinking, and how it has become established as a fact in the present century.

We hear echoes of this faith in many forms. In the inauguration address of President Kennedy (1917-1963), he stated: "Ask not what your country can do for you; ask what you can do for your country." This was lauded by the press. It is true that we should not be entirely dependent upon our country. But it is also true in a free country, such as ours, that the nation can never take the place of God, nor provide us with those inalienable rights such as "life, liberty, and the pursuit of happiness," for these are gifts of the Creator. It may not make an absolute demand of us.

The question raised by the Pharisees and the Herodians: "Is it lawful to give tribute unto Caesar, or not?" was answered by Jesus in a practical way. He took a Roman coin and asked whose image was on it. When they answered, "Caesar's," He said, "Render therefore unto Caesar the things which are Caesar's, and unto God the things that are God's" (Matt. 22:15-22). Jesus, you will recall, turned the tables on His questioners. They had tried to hang Him on the horns of a dilemma. The Herodians recognized Caesar as divine; the Pharisees said only God was divine. Now they, and we, are left with that same question: Who is worthy of our tribute, or faith? The answer is given by Jesus at His trial before Pilate. Pilate boasted of his power to crucify Him. This was the power of Caesar, delegated to him as Governor of Judea. To this Jesus replied, "Thou couldest have no power *at all* against

me, except it were given thee from above" (John 19:11).
This is in line with His earlier answer: "My kingdom is
not of this world" (John 18:36).

Our reply, as Christians, to the belief that we are
only products of our society is a reasonable one. "Yes,
indeed," we may say, "we are, in part, products of our
genes and environment. But we are much more than
that. We are created by God, and *re-created* by the work
of Jesus, our Lord. We are citizens of this country. But
we are also citizens of that kingdom, which is not of
this world, and which is ruled over by Jesus, the
Christ, and none other. We cannot accept your faith
that we are social products planned by behavioral
engineers and committees of government experts. We
are not products. You are thinking of things such as
Ford motor cars. We are God's children, and brothers
and sisters of Jesus, and each other."

One of the best satires on the social product theory is
George Orwell's *Animal Farm*. Pigs lead a revolt of
the farm animals against the farmer and his family,
who are destroyed. Gradually the pigs begin to look
and act like those they had deposed. They become the
same. They can add nothing new to the scene. They can
rise no higher than the society which conditions them.
The tragic figure in this story is Old Dobbin, the horse.
He is worked to death by the pigs who became
farmers, because they treat him more harshly.
Although they do, he gives them his blind obedience.
IIe pays his tribute to them.

When you question this belief in class, you are likely
to be regarded as a reactionary. Someone or other is
sure to quote B.F. Skinner to you. But don't worry.
Jesus' question leaves no one at rest.

4. *Man, you're sick.* This is not the judgment of

your friend upon you, but the belief of those who adhere to the psychopathological view of human beings. It is the synthesis of nineteenth-century thought, particularly that exemplified by Darwin, Marx and Freud. As we have shown earlier, the optimism of humanism always ends in despair. From man, the Lord of the universe, to man, the sniveling idiot, is the inevitable movement.

We remember that sin does not enter into the formula of humanism. Then how do we explain that human beings have not really been getting better in every way day by day. At least not all of them. People are sick and they need physicians, surgeons and particularly psychiatrists. Nations go to war with other nations. Riches change hands, but the poor still have their faces ground into the earth (polluted, of course). People do not act rationally. They become traitors, criminals, dissidents, rebels.

What could have gone wrong?

Oh, just a little sickness that will be cured.

What caused the sickness?

Nothing to worry about. The evolutionary process is derailed. But only temporarily, of course. We'll soon get it back on its tracks.

What happened?

Ran into a *cul-de-sac*, that's what! The old biological urge lost its way when it produced man. He, you see, did this silly thing of producing his own environment. Artificial, of course. Generally goes by the name of civilization.

But how could civilization be responsible for this? It is supposed to be good. My professor in history 301 tells me that's what it is all about. This is what we come to university to study.

Oh, yes, of course, but accidents happen now and then. We must expect one once in a while, now, must we not? After all, the earth is twenty billion years old, but man is only—let me see—what, a million years or so.

That seems a long time to me!

I suppose it does when you are young. But remember a lot has happened in that time. We began in the primordial soup. And now we are almost there.

Where?

At the top, of course.

Like New York City?

Better than that. Few things to do yet. Get them done soon. If we can put a man on the moon, we are bound to straighten up the earth.

How?

We are working on that. Be patient. It won't take us long. Had the old boys of other years known what we know now, things would have been different.

We wouldn't be sick, is that it?

Yes. Had there been experts available, they could have worked things out. We have all this malfunctioning, and despair, because things got a bit mixed up.

How mixed up?

The brain, for example. Pretty important, wouldn't you agree? It is still a bit of a mess. There is a bit of it that we have inherited from the reptiles, another from the simians, another from our childhood, and so on. They tend to short circuit each other. Then there is the bicameral thing; the two compartments of the brain. Left and right. The left is the up-to-date side. This is where we work out problems and math formulas. Pretty important. It is the rational thing. The right is the problem. That is for right-handed people, and *vice-versa*. In the old days, people were bicameral. The right side of their brain dominated the left. They heard voices and thought God was speaking to them.

So God is merely the right hemisphere?

I didn't say that. But I suppose that is the case. You'll observe that as rationality increases, God decreases. That is why we never use that name anymore.

But then we're not sick?

No. I mean, yes. We have a conflict of memories. Childhood memories, ancient memories, very ancient memories. That sort of thing. Then our social environment frustrates us, inhibits us. Our primary drives are misdirected. Our feelings are thwarted. We do not react as we should to evolutionary change.

Is there nothing we can do about it?

Oh, yes. See your psychiatrist! She'll help you to examine your memories and show you which ones are depressing you.

You mean she'll treat me as someone who is all screwed up?

Only in a manner of speaking.

Is there nothing else we can do?

Get rid of the past, and start again!

As simple as that?

Yes. Come back tomorrow, and I'll show you my plans.

These are four very general views of "man" that pervade campus thought. I have mentioned them in the hope that they will enable you to discern the "man" of the moment, either in your class or in your reading. What you have been told about "man" is likely to be one of, or a mixture of, all four. And what you may have learned from secular sources will not help you to know who you are, why you are, or what you exist for. You will have nothing to hold on to, but a few words.

Before going on to the Christian answer, let me quote from Aleksandr Solzhenitsyn's Harvard address, of June 8, 1978, for what he says shows how the measure of a man or a woman has been lost.

> As humanism in its development became more and more materialistic, it made itself increasingly accessible to speculation and manipulation at first by socialism and then by communism. So that Karl Marx was able to say in 1844 that "communism is naturalized humanism!" This statement turned out to be not entirely senseless. One does see the same stones in the foundations of a despiritualized humanism and of any type of socialism; endless materialism; freedom from religion and religious responsibility, which under communist regimes reach the state of anti-religious dictatorship. . . . Not by coincidence all of communism's meaningless pledges and oaths are about Man, with a capital M, and his earthly happiness.

Do not be upset by this discovery of Solzhenitsyn. His Christian faith was hammered out on the anvil of suffering. When we look around us, we see the consequences of human pride. Life without God is not life at all. It is a dull, dreary existence in which individuals are stripped of their uniqueness, and treated as objects to be processed by means of computers, as meaningless things with no more identity then their Social Security numbers. They are the helpless victims of the IRS, the FBI, the CIA, credit companies and nasty little committees that a confused and stupid bureaucracy appoints to control us lest we discover we were created to be free.

As a Christian, you know there is only one way of measuring ourselves and finding out who we are, and that is through Jesus, who is the way and the truth of life—by giving us our new identity as His kinsfolk. Along with St. Paul we know, ". . . if any man be in Christ, he is a new creature: old things are passed away; behold, all things are become new" (2 Cor. 5:17).

By contrast with humanism, the Christian faith has so much to say that is positive and hopeful about human beings.

8

God's Exaltation
of Men and Women

This is a good note on which to begin a chapter on Christian anthropology. The story of God in His relationship with His creatures is one that exalts them. This is true all the way from creation to the cross.

We have noted in an earlier chapter that God chose to create Adam, the first man. "And God said, Let us make man in our image, after our likeness: and let them have dominion . . ." (Gen. 1:26).

When we pause to be still in the divine presence, we become aware that our awareness of God makes us unique. It marks us as those who are distinctively apart from the rest of creation. We are conscious of ourselves, and the creation of which we are part. We think; we have ideas; we have the will to express those ideas, both in words and actions. Because we do, we communicate with each other. We have concepts of truth, goodness and beauty that transcend the knowledge gained by sensory perception. Not only do we enjoy works of art, we find them necessary for our individual and communal well-being.

We have, above all, the capacity to give our loyalty to someone or something. This is what religion is all about. No anthropology is complete that ignores man as *homo religiosus*. The test of a human being is what he or she worships. We become like that to which we ascribe ultimate worth. If it is money, we become misers. If it is Jesus, we become His kinsfolk.

Not only are we unique because of the uniqueness of our creation. We are unique because God has created us for fellowship with himself. The biblical model is that of the covenant God made with Abraham. Adam is the first living soul, but Abraham, surely, is the first to express the nature of the relationship to which he, and everyone, is called. The covenant initiated by God is one of trust. The keynote is: God is faithful.

It is by understanding the mystery and grandeur of this unique relationship that we understand the meaning of morality. Because the *Covenanter* is holy, the *covenantee* is invited to be holy as well: to be perfect even as our Father in Heaven is perfect. By repentance, we turn, or rather return, to God. In doing so, we become increasingly sensitive to the divine imperative. The articulation of this imperative is found in the Decalogue, the moral challenge of the prophets, and in Jesus who is the personal expression of the divine challenge and its response.

Of Sin and Bondage

The story told in the Old Testament is our story as well as that of the ancient Israelites. From it we learn of God's faithfulness on the one hand, and of human disobedience on the other. Because of the latter we are estranged from one another. Along with Adam and Eve we participate in the Fall. The first sin is the desire to be "as gods, knowing good and evil." What does this mean but self-centered existence! Without God at the center of our lives, we lose our innocence. I think we also lose the sense of joy and thankfulness. Like Adam we are left naked, alone and alienated. As Adam and Eve became aliens, or strangers, in God's

Garden, so do we. Once they were aware of the difference between right and wrong, they left the center of the Garden and tried to hide in the darkness of the shadows among the trees on the perimeter.

In the late afternoon when the sun was low and a breeze cooled the land, we read of how God came walking in His Garden. It is a beautiful picture. He comes in fellowship, but His friends are not there. He calls, "Adam, Adam, where art thou?" Because Adam is called by name, he hears and knows who he is. What happens because of this hearing?

He is afraid.

Does not this tell the story of all godless people? They are afraid. In fear they live in the shadows, build prisons for themselves in the name of security, and live in enmity with their wives or husbands, with their children and with their neighbors. Even humanists must recognize the accuracy of this portrayal of the human condition. The evidence is all around us. It is the evidence of sin.

According to the Genesis 3 account of the Fall, we may conclude that sin results in:

disobedience
bondage
estrangement
hostility
fear
illusion.

As most of you are familiar with sin, both theologically and existentially, I would like to touch upon the last characteristic—that of *illusion*. I find that this best describes the human situation of our time. The humanists have repeated the first sin: that of pride, the pride of being as God. The sins of the flesh are very small ones indeed compared with this ghastly sin of the will.

Jesus, we remember, made His home with the lawless, the landless and the outsiders. For doing so, His moral authority was discredited by the Pharisees and the scribes. These were the pious, religious people of those days. Yet these were the ones Jesus denounced. Why? Because they set themselves up as gods to others. They loaded them with heavy burdens; they were indifferent to the plight of the overburdened; they made a great show of being religious, and lorded it over lesser mortals. (It is all there in Matthew 23.)

In our day the humanists have replaced the Pharisees and scribes and have tried to load people with inexorable burdens. Their religion is, therefore, one which creates bondage.

One of the best analyses of this sin of pride, and its illusions, may be found in Christopher Booker's book, *The Neophiliacs*, published in this country in 1969 by Gambit, Inc. I refer to it at length because it is not well known. I think it was too intelligent, too challenging and too Christian to attract the attention of most booksellers and critics.

Mr. Booker is not a professional theologian. He is a man of his times. After his graduation from Cambridge, he identified with the bright young men of the fifties and sixties. He was an editor and journalist with cutting wit. One of his TV review shows, which panned the establishment, was "That Was the Week That Was."

As a man of his times, he paused to reflect upon them. In his reflection, he realized that England, and the West generally, had been caught up in a huge "collective fantasy-self." This madness was in full display in the sixties. He gives us a splendid review of what may only be classified as a Mad Hatter's Tea Party.

The Bishop of Woolwich gives evidence of this in

Regina vs. Penguin Books, Ltd., 1960: "What I think is clear is that what Lawrence is trying to do is to portray the sex relationship as something essentially sacred . . . as in a real sense an act of body communion."

Professor George Carstairs, BBC Reith Lecturer, 1962-63, wrote: "A new concept is emerging of sexual relationships as a source of pleasure."

Prime Minister Harold Wilson said: "This is our message for the sixties—a Socialist-inspired scientific and technological revolution releasing energy on an enormous scale."

John Lennon, of the Beatles, proclaimed: "We're more popular than Jesus now."

And many more examples which, alas, too few recognize as folly.

He recounts the follies of the pundits, and the popular heroes, to show it is part of human nature to escape from reality into a dream world that reinforces vanity, greed, violence, lust. From such a mad situation there is no escape except through death. Those who indulge in rebellion against God are caught in the grip of fantasy which drives them onward in a mounting spiral of absurd demands.

Basing his analysis on Jung's interpretation, he postulates a five-stage cycle of prideful existence beginning:

1. At *The Anticipation Stage*, the ego-asserting drive pushes restraining authorities aside to indulge in self-centered fantasies.

2. *The Dream Stage* follows as the fantasy becomes the controlling ideal. For a time, all seems to go well. Illusions are satisfied, and lusts are gratified. An example of this is Nabokov's *Lolita*. The young girl's mother is run over most conveniently so that the guardian of Lolita is liberated to enjoy a forbidden sexual

relationship. One that he has dreamed about regularly. This illicit relationship becomes a wild sexual Odyssey that leads from motel to motel. The anticipated delights of this erotic fantasy, however, are blighted by a frustration which seems to be inexplicable.

3. This is *The Frustration Stage*. At this stage the victim of his self-centered fantasy attempts furiously to preserve his cherished dream. As a consequence, he craves the most violent sensations. What began, thus, as a romance, becomes destructive depravity.

4. *The Nightmare Stage*, therefore, follows. This is the complete reversal of the Dream Stage. All that was anticipated eagerly is turned upside down. A feeling of morbid dread prevails. The world is possessed by the powers of darkness; the times are out of joint. To such an experience of disharmony there is only one solution:

5. *The Death Wish Stage*, or final explosion into reality, judgment, condemnation and self-destruction.

This five-fold pattern of original sin is common to the great literature of the West. We see examples of it in *Romeo and Juliet*, *Doctor Faustus* and *Tristan and Isolde*.

"We are such things as dreams are made of," is well-testified to by the actions of societies and individuals. It is seen in Cain, Babel, King David's son Absalom, Judas Iscariot, William the Conqueror and Richard M. Nixon. What more frightening illustrations are there of this sin than the history of Alexander the Great, the Caesars, Napoleon, Lenin and Stalin, Mussolini and Hitler? Fantasies are nurtured in the seedbed of the unconscious. They are usually regarded as harmless, although they end in controlling events, thereby resulting in the tragic existence of the Fall.

An excellent summing up of this fallen condition is to be found in Isaiah's story of Lucifer (Isa. 14), and in the second Psalm, where the Psalmist observes the illusions of those in power and remarks: "He that sitteth in the heavens shall laugh: the Lord shall have them in derision" (Ps. 2:4).

I have indicated that Christopher Booker is not a professional theologian. What he is is a man of this prideful twentieth century, a brilliant product of an ancient university, who has come to take the measure of himself, and his civilization, according to God's revelation in Jesus. When one reads his book, one may trace how he moves from a chronicler of events to being a philosopher who tries to find an underlying pattern of meaning beneath the confusion and follies of his day. But human reason is insufficient to provide an answer. He thus moves on to be a theologian grasped by grace. He concludes his analysis by showing that Jesus was the only one to face the pattern and consequences of evil. The fantasy cycle of the state and temple is enacted in the drama of Jesus' passion. By the execution of Jesus, the fantasy-controlled leaders presume they have destroyed the man who threatens their pride and the institutions built upon it. Evil men, however, could not negate God's purpose fulfilled by Jesus. "On Easter morning comes the Resurrection, completing the full cycle of the perfect man: who had acted out the pattern of the world's sins, and yet was reborn."

I think Booker's position is one which is enormously helpful in showing the human scene as one of sin and bondage. It is a repetition of the Fall. The Neophiliacs are, of course, those who love the new world of the future, which still has to be built. This world of pride's construction was well envisioned by Aldous Huxley in *Brave New World* and by George Orwell in *1984*. It is the world of illusion. To understand the real world, we have to begin with God and our relationship to Him.

Before I began this chapter, I received an unexpected letter from an alumnus who had graduated eight years ago. From university he went on to law school, and from there to business where he achieved immediate success. But he did not write to tell me of this. Instead he wrote to tell me that he had resigned. He did so because he discovered he was losing his soul in a world of riches and fantasy. It was this world that had been upheld as the desirable one during his campus years. He was black, and he had grown up in Harlem. He writes:

> I found that the self-fulfilling prophecy of failure, typical of any minority person with low SAT scores was finally negated by my success. I had achieved the goal set for me by my liberal professors. But it was nothing. I thought now was the time to pocket my ego and begin again. So, I submitted my letter of resignation, not caring about the consequences of unemployment. I hope to realize the goals of Christian fellowship, which others had found, and shared with me in my times of need. In retrospect I see it was this fellowship that was the only moral support I had to help me overcome the spiritually deadening experience of being "a token minority" caught in the dynamics of an ascending economic and social mobility in a society which values a man by his possessions rather than by the commitment of his heart.

This testimony reinforces the reality of the Fall. To turn from God is to turn to darkness, despair and death. We dig our own graves with the shovel of pride, and build our own death cells with the bricks and cement of our self-indulgent fantasies. Whatever the faults of the atheistic existentialists, such as Sartre, Camus and

Beckett, they reminded us that godless existence is a life of sin and bondage.

We are responsible because we are responsive.
This is what sin demonstrates. The Fall means a fall from our origin, and, therefore, from our destiny. Is not this what the parable of the Prodigal Son is all about? That young rascal disowns his origin by demanding his inheritance. It is given to him by his father without complaint. The son goes to "sin city," in the wasteland, and there dissipates his wealth. His good-time friends desert him. He is so alienated that the only place he can go to is a pigsty. What a grim end for a proud young Jew! It is in the pigsty that he comes to himself. He realizes he is responsible for his miserable condition.

This recognition of his personal responsibility reminds him, however, that he has an origin—one that is good. Seeking to reclaim it, in the hope that he will have the same advantages as the slaves, he returns home. When he comes within sight of the farm, he is spotted by his dad, who has been waiting for him. To his great surprise his dad rushes to meet him, embraces him and claims him as his beloved son.

The position of the prodigal son is now infinitely greater than it was, even before he left home. Now he is sure of two things: his dad's love, and his love for his dad. In recovering his origin, he is given his destiny.

Just as it was Jesus who told this parable, so is it He who reveals our true selves in revealing God. By doing so, we become aware of who we are, and for whom we exist. Our own sin is the evidence of our failure to be responsive to God and, therefore, responsible to Him and to His people. The human situation, by itself, is in opposition to the perfect manhood of Jesus. By Him we are judged. But, by Him, we are also redeemed and set free to respond in love to our Father's love.

When we speak of the total depravity of man, it is this of which we speak. It does not mean we are hopelessly lost. It means there is no faculty in us which may be separated from another and regarded as absolute. The rational view of man, for example, seizes hold of reason as the divine principle and tries to absolutize it. Educators are tempted to do the same. Professors may give you a mark of 100 in a course. But no one is at that level of performance in the university of life. "For all have sinned, and come short of the glory of God" (Rom. 3:23).

The exaltation of human beings

This is not something we do for ourselves, and by ourselves. It is the work of God through the activity of the Holy Spirit.

Earlier I suggested that the story of God's people in the Old Testament is the story of us all. It is a story with an unhappy ending if left to itself. But the Good News is that the human story of failure has been taken into the divine story with the happy ending.

St. Paul tells us that in the fullness, or completion, of time, "God sent forth his Son, made of a woman, made under the law, to redeem them that were under the law, that we might receive the adoption of sons" (Gal. 4:4, 5). This moment of creation's completion is the Incarnation. The beauty of this saving act is demonstrated by the birth narratives of St. Matthew and St. Luke. They tell of the final preparation of this event. Mary's obedient response to the revelation of the Holy Spirit's work within her is testified to by her *Magnificat* (her praise to God). It is clear that she understood the work of her promised Son to be that of exalting His people: "He hath put down the mighty from their seats, and exalted them of low degree. He hath filled the hungry with good things; the rich he hath sent empty away" (Luke 1:52, 53).

The place of this exaltation defies human imagination. Where was it? On the cross! Thus, St. John writes, "Now is the judgment of this world: now shall the prince of this world be cast out. And I, if I be lifted up from the earth, will draw all men unto me. This he said, signifying what death he should die" (John 12:31-33).

This death, in turn, is the evidence of God's love for the world. It is the New Covenant. The old one, made with Abraham, was broken by those for whom it was established. We could say it was so broken that nothing less than this costly new one was sufficient to assure people that God's love is so limitless that it reaches from creation to the cross. As Jesus told Nicodemus, *now we know God,* for He has revealed himself to us face to face. His face bears His smile of welcome. We who have chosen the far country, on the other side of Eden, are invited to the place of honor in the heart of God.

Jesus bore our defeats on the cross and turned them into victory. This is the theme of the first sermon ever preached by a minister of the new church after Pentecost. It is contained in these words of St. Peter: "This Jesus hath God raised up, whereof we all are witnesses. Therefore being by the right hand of God exalted, and having received of the Father the promise of the Holy Ghost, he hath shed forth this, which ye now see and hear" (Acts 2:32, 33).

In this light we see that the Church is the place on earth where Christ's work of exaltation continues. We are born as individuals controlled by our genes and environment. We are born again as children of God with a new identity. Our part in this act of exaltation is to accept our salvation and work it out in fear and trembling.

I find it difficult to improve upon St. Paul's summing up of our Lord's work, as he writes of it in Romans 5:12-21, and 1 Corinthians 15:20-26. What was lost in the first Adam is restored with a fulfillment-plus by the second Adam. In Colossians and Hebrews, we read that Jesus is "the image of the invisible God." What Adam was called to be was fulfilled through Jesus, the obedient Son. In order to understand this more fully, I think it is well to reexamine the biblical doctrine of the *imago Dei.*

The Image of God

Until recently the belief that men and women are unique was based upon the revealed evidence contained in the book of Genesis. When the embryonic UNESCO met in Paris in 1948 to compose a charter of human rights, the non-Communist delegates included this phrase, *image of God,* as the basis for their support of human dignity. The Russian delegate, Professor Pavlov, headed a group which classified this belief as antiquated and reactionary. His criticism was summed up in these words, which represent the belief in man as a social product: "Freedom and equality in rights are not inherent by birth but are a product of social structure."

There are only five references to the image of God in the Old Testament. They are all in Genesis. Three of these are in the first chapter, one in the fifth, and one in the ninth. The first three affirm man as God's unique creation—male and female. This uniqueness is classified in terms of three responsibilities, that of:
  a. bearing rule on the earth.
  b. being fruitful.
  c. replenishing the earth.

The fourth reference affirms Adam as our common ancestor: "On the day when God created man, he made him in the likeness of God. He created them male and female, and on the day when he created them, he blessed them and called them man" (Gen. 5:1, 2 NEB).

The fifth reference, in the ninth chapter, bases our moral accountability for the life of each other on the foundation of the *imago Dei*.

All of these references point to the mystery of being human. *To be in God's image and likeness is to be a reflector of the ultimate mystery*. It is, therefore, *to be responsible*.

The five references underline this truth:

1. The first, Genesis 1:26, includes the command *to bear rule over all God's creatures*. Some humanists have chosen to interpret this to mean "exploit." All the ecological ills of our time are, therefore, laid at its doorstep. Would God make such an insane command? To bear rule in His image is to rule with Him, and for Him. It is to be *responsible:* for this means exercising authority. We are created bearing the image of the *auctor*—the author, the initiator, the creator. To be so created is to be an authentic human being. It is *to be:* to be in our own right, because it is a right divinely bestowed upon us. It is not to be in the image of society which was not there at creation.

To rule with the author of life is *to care*. And to care is to be responsible for God's creatures over which human beings are to rule.

One moment a young wife is free, frolicsome and flirtatious. Nine months later—give or take a week or two—and she is lovingly anxious, concerned, protective. Why? Because she has become a mother. One who has been given the responsibility of exercising moral authority in her home. So responsibly may she accept this role that she may overrule her husband for the sake of her daughter or son.

In this same way, we are privileged to bear rule for "all creatures great and small." By doing so, we are involved in the sacramental unity of the human and non-human. The antonym for rule, by the way, is not no rule, but misrule. And who is the lord of misrule, but Beelzebub, the prince of chaos.

To understand fully the nature of the rule we have to bear, we have to look to the cross. It was there God's authority was completely revealed. The rule shunned by the first Adam is borne by the second Adam.

2. We are *to be fruitful* and increase. This was the obvious directive to give at the beginning of things. We may well have reached the stage where we are to do less procreating and more caring. If we, as human beings, learn to care more for each other, and for the earth, we may be assured of a different and, perhaps, better form of fruitfulness. The task of Adam was to be a husband. The word "husband" means cultivating, tending, caring, managing prudently or carefully. This meaning is reinforced by the third call to responsibility.

3. That of *replenishing the earth*. We replenish as husbandmen or gardeners. The clue to the faithful discharge of this responsibility lies in our obedience. Our disobedience turns the garden into a wasteland. We can reap it or rape it, treasure it or tear it apart for its fossilized fuels and gems, and leave it like a city garbage dump.

We are all too well aware of the consequences of mankind's disobedience. Technocracy—the rule of the machine—has tried to manufacture people in its own image. And it has done so in the name of Utopias—no-places—still to be constructed. Commenting upon this, Professor Charles Birch wrote in a report of the World

Council of Churches, "The pursuit of illusory paradise leads to eco-catastrophe. The history of eco-catastrophes is the history of the human race replacing sustainable societies with unsustainable ones. . . . There can be no sort of age in the future unless we conform to some of the rules that were observed in getting us here. . . . If the life of the world is to be sustained and renewed, as directed in Genesis, it will have to be with a new sort of science and technology governed by a new sort of economics and politics."

But where may our gigantic technocracies find the power of renewal? This is the question the Church has to take seriously and to risk answering.

4. The fourth facet of responsibility is our responsibility for each other as male and female. This is what sex is all about. There are two sexes, but only one *divine image*. This image transcends physical and organic limitations.

The economic and political exploitation of the earth is also reflected in sexual exploitation. Throughout history women have been the slaves of masculine sexual fantasies. In Jesus' time, a widow or divorcee had no means of support. She was forced by the laws of economic necessity to sell her body to the lustful men of her village. Jesus not only defended such women, but loved them. It was of one of them that our Lord said, "Her sins, which are many, are forgiven; for she loved much" (Luke 7:47). During the days of the Anglo-Saxons, once an owner made his female slave pregnant, he sold her as a prostitute. Today a woman's sexuality is reduced to the centerfold of pornographic magazines. In other words, the divine image is ignored. What a far cry this is from: "In the day that God created man, in the likeness of God made he him; male and female created he them: and blessed them, and called their name Adam." It is interesting to note that the word "Adam" is used here in its generic sense; that is, it is the name of all men and women, for all are equally human.

It was with a sense of the New Testament's exaltation of women that Robert Burns wrote:

Auld Nature swears, the lovely dears
Her noblest work she classes, O:
Her prentice han' she try'd on man,
An' then she made the lasses, O,
Green grow the rashes, O;
Green grow the rashes, O;
The sweetest hours that e'er I spend,
Are spent among the lasses, O.

5. Although the *imago Dei* is universal, it is also particular. The life of each individual is sacred:

Whoso sheddeth man's blood,
by man shall his blood be shed:
for in the image of God made he man. (Gen. 9:6)

This statement is hard to understand. Governments have used it to justify capital punishment. And it seems to do this very thing. I think, however, that it is more complex in its meaning.

Cain killed his brother, Abel. When he confessed his sin, he said, "Anyone who meets me can kill me." God's answer was, "If anyone kills Cain, Cain shall be avenged sevenfold. So the Lord put a mark on Cain, in order that anyone meeting him *should not* kill him." Although Cain had ignored God's image in Abel, God had not ignored his image in Cain. On the contrary, he put another mark on him. He was branded as a fallen man whose life was to be spared.

From my perspective, I perceive that the killing of

the killer initiates the cycle of death in which civilizations are imprisoned. This passage introduces us to ourselves as citizens of a guilty world who have loved death too much, and life too little.

The biblical evidence is clear. Our human life is given to us to be cherished. The meaning of the fifth *imago Dei* is given to us in the Sermon on the Mount:

> Ye have heard that it hath been said,
> An eye for an eye,
> And a tooth for a tooth:
> But I say unto you,
> That ye resist not evil . . .
> Love your enemies,
> bless them that curse you,
> do good to them that hate you,
> and pray for them
> which despitefully use you. (Matt. 5:38-44)

This teaching is hard to accept. It is bound to be. It is the Lord's! His meaning is made further plain by His quiet words to His disciples in the Garden of Gethsemane, "Put up again thy sword . . . for all they that take the sword shall perish with the sword" (Matt. 26:52). This surely has been demonstrated by the history of the rise and decline of civilizations.

Both the fifth *imago Dei* and Jesus' words in the garden raise an interesting moral point: Who grants amnesty to the politicians who use the sword, that is, those who commit others to its use?

The evidence of the Bible is powerful: to be human is to be responsible, awfully responsible. We have seen this lived by the man who was completely human. Civil, military and ecclesiastical powers committed the ultimate sin, the ultimate violation of their responsibility for life, by executing Him. The whole of creation, St.

Luke tells us, wept in pain and horror. There, on that cross, the ultimate responsibility was revealed. The Rule of God was declared as the Rule of Life.

To be in the imago Dei *is to live in community.*

The humanist beliefs about man eventually assert the collective society, and in doing so deny the authenticity of individuals.

We have noted that man is unique because of his creation by the Word of God. As Christians, we are given our name at baptism to indicate that we are known individually to God, so well known that He counts the hairs of our head. In His sight, we are infinitely precious.

Our individual uniqueness, however, is also a corporate, or communal, uniqueness. Just as Adam and Eve were created for each other, so are we. The stages of awareness are perhaps more obvious these days than they have ever been.

a. As citizens of the state, we are isolated by laws and their threats, and left to exist in anxiety. The more we trust bureaucracies, the more alienated we feel. It is exactly the same position as Adam after the Fall.

b. We are born as citizens, but by God's grace we are reborn into the fullness of the glorious liberty of the children of God. Our liberty now transcends that which St. Paul knew as a Roman citizen, and I as an American. Our mortal existence has its uniqueness in the corporate life of the Church. This is one of the messages of the experience of Pentecost. We come to Christ one by one. In His presence, however, we find each other. To do this, we lay aside our prides, our prejudices and our loneliness. By the activity of the Holy Spirit, we become of one mind and heart. By doing so, we learn not to esteem ourselves as better than anyone else. The letters of the New Testament spell it all out for us. We are many, and different, members of the same Body. The ankle may not think it likes the toe, or the forefinger that it likes the thumb, but the ankle and the forefinger have a hard time of it without the toe or the thumb. When we leave the judgment to God, we discover how beautiful are the other parts of the Body and how dependent we are upon them. To be a Christian is *to be in the Church.*

By having our *imago Dei* restored to us, *we have our being in community.* For this we are created, and called. What is the community of Christians anyway, but the communion of love? I hope I made this clear in my diagram of the triangle with Jesus at the center. In other words, the fullness of life is known in community: in the community of Jesus which is turned to the world to share the divine love with it.

The history of man and salvation-history

I pointed out earlier that there is no meaning in history if our faith in Jesus as God's Word is denied. If there is no meaning, people have no uniqueness, and history is pointless. At its best, it is but a record of "matter in motion." And that as an answer leaves a great deal to be desired: for who is it that is aware of this, and why?

St. Paul's declaration that Jesus was born in God's time—*kairos*—tells us at least two things:

a. That up to this point, history had not been fulfilled or completed. It was in a state of waiting, a state of expectancy. Some found this waiting too much and too long for them so they turned to law, or revolutionary politics, or despair. These were the Israelites who gave up their heritage of trust in the living God. Among them were those who rejected Moses' prophetic ministry, concentrated upon him as the lawmaker, and called themselves his disciples. There were those who tried to confine God to the cultic practices of the Temple. And there were those who, in their despair, turned their faces to Rome and accepted it as divine. We could compare them to contemporary humanists.

It was, surely, of them that St. John the Beloved said, "He came unto his own, but his own received him not" (John 1:11). Yet, there were those, as we have seen, who waited in expectancy—Elizabeth, Mary, Joseph, Ann, Simeon, the poor landless people, the disciples. Because they waited attentively, they recognized Jesus as their Lord and Liberator, who was the fulfillment of history.

b. The preaching, proclamation, and teaching of the Church that was born at Pentecost affirmed that God's purpose in history was completed by Jesus. For those who waited attentively, Jesus' birth was like the bells of heaven ringing out God's victory over the limitations of time and space. His purpose in creation was completed in Jesus who was born in Bethlehem at the time of Caesar Augustus and executed outside the walls of Jerusalem during the governorship of Pontius Pilate.

It was the response of the first disciples to this revelation that characterized the unique witness of the Church and the unique nature of Christian thought. Altogether it was a great affirmation of human worth. The ways of evil men and their governments could not prevent the fulfillment of God's loving purpose for mankind. His ways were clearly revealed through Jesus. By His redemption of the world, He had redeemed time as well as people and space. No wonder the outcasts, the outlaws and the outsiders responded so readily to this good news of their exaltation.

Turn again to the sixth and seventh chapters of Acts. It is the account of the appointment of the seven deacons, and the execution of the first martyr who witnessed to this truth both by his life and by his death. We read of how the synagogue of the Libertines (that is, the Hellenistic Jews in Jerusalem), was so opposed to the proclamation of this good news that its members manufactured a "fixed trial" with false witnesses. The case for the prosecution was based upon the charge: "We have heard [Stephen] say, that this Jesus of Nazareth shall destroy this place [the Temple], and shall change the customs which Moses delivered us" (Acts 6:14).

At his trial before the High Priest, Stephen rested his case upon the historical acts initiated by God. He began with Abraham's response to the divine glory, and went on to record God's saving deeds which culminated in "the coming of the Just One; of whom ye have been now the betrayers and murderers" (Acts 7:52).

This great declaration of salvation-history was based upon the Church's understanding of God the Father, who revealed himself in liberating and saving acts for His people, thereby affirming His love for them.

When we look at the Letter to the Hebrews, we see how sure the early Church was of this salvation-history—so sure that the writer of the letter could speak for every Christian by saying, "How shall we escape, if we neglect so great salvation?" (Heb. 2:3). The whole of this splendid letter is a testimony to the work and ministry of Jesus: for by them the people who believe in Him are exalted. No wonder slaves, women and outcasts flocked to those first communities of Christian faith. It was there, for the first time, they heard that the news from God was good. There was a royal place for everyone. Thus, St. Peter wrote, "Ye are a chosen generation, a royal priesthood . . . which in time past were not a people, but are now the people of God" (1 Pet. 2:9, 10).

Citizens of Two Realms

God's saving work transcends space and time, laws and control systems, pride and physical power. We are aware of this by our trust in Jesus who is Lord above all. This act of transcendence, it is important to remember, occurs *in* space and time, and *in* people of flesh and desire. We are individuals, and citizens of particular countries, who are reborn as citizens of the eternal realm, not by the flesh, but, "of water and of the Spirit" (John 3:5). We remember, once again, how Jesus claimed that His kingdom was not of this world, in His trial by Pontius Pilate. Jesus gave no material rewards to His followers; no places of honor in his royal court; no bribes; no decorations and titles. It may be hard for us to understand this. We are conditioned to believe that if you are good, you will be rewarded. To be rewarded, of course, means candy and Cadillacs, and castles, and endless credit.

The disciples learned slowly what the new life Jesus offered them was all about. The sons of Zebedee, James and John, asked for the positions of authority at the left and right hand of Jesus when He ascended His throne. Patiently, Jesus taught them, and the rest of the disciples, that "whosoever of you will be the chiefest, shall be servant of all. For even the Son of man came not to be ministered unto, but to minister, and to give his live as a ransom for many" (Mark 10:44, 45).

Our Lord's life and death are one act by which all worldly power is subordinated to the ultimate power of the divine love. God, that is, reveals His power by refusing to use the power of armies of men and of angels (Matt. 26:53).

184

The Gospel of St. John makes it clear that the power of God is not in the cultic practices of the Temple; nor in the written Torah; nor in the sacred well of Jacob in Samaria; nor in the pagan healing pool of Bethesda (John 5:2-5). Where then is this divine power and glory? There is only one answer: in Jesus! Remember how He told the Samaritan woman at Jacob's well that history was fulfilled in Him? Through Him authentic worshipers "worship the Father in spirit and in truth: for the Father seeketh such to worship him. God is a Spirit: and they that worship him must worship him in spirit and in truth" (John 4:23, 24). Jesus then went on to tell the woman that He was the Messiah, or Christ, the one come from God to be His face—the face in which the divine glory is seen.

Once again we affirm that God has come to us in the flesh that we who are in the flesh may come to Him. As citizens of the flesh, we become citizens of the eternal city, "the city of the living God, the heavenly Jerusalem" (Heb. 12:22). Although we are in the flesh, subject to its weaknesses, we are in the spirit, subject to its transforming power.

I can verify this from my own experience, particularly that in the prisoner of war camp of Chungkai, Thailand. I, and others like me, were defeated in the flesh. Indeed, there was very little flesh left on most of us. At one time, I could span my waist with my two hands. In the death house, in a death camp, new life came to me as a dying man. How? By the work of the Holy Spirit, the action of grace! God breathed into the dying bodies of a dying society of men, and there was a resurrection. We then lived by the Spirit. By the Spirit, miracles happened. A garbage heap of death was transformed into a sacrament of life.

I find it essential to remember that the power of the

Holy Spirit is active in, and through, the bruised and wounded flesh of individuals, and in the visible Body of Christ of which they are members. During the time of our education for life, we are in the flesh. The flesh is weak. As we grow weaker in the flesh, however, we grow stronger in the spirit, by faith in Jesus. The miracle of true substantiation is that flesh is transformed into spirit: and by the spirit we live. Part of this miracle is that the fruits, or works, of the spirit are done in the flesh. The Holy Spirit uses our flesh for the purpose of feeding the hungry, clothing the naked, liberating the captives, befriending the lonely, helping the weak and supporting the helpless.

It is the community of the Holy Spirit that makes possible—not only possible, but joyful—our fleshly existence.

We have a dual citizenship, both of which are operative at the same time. Although we are in the world, we are "pilgrims and strangers" because it can never be home. As a minister to a university, I find I am constantly aware of my weaknesses, both physical and intellectual. Too many criticisms, too many mental battles, and all the ills that the flesh is heir to, leave me exhausted at times. Exhausted, but not defeated. New strength for the day's tasks come through the spirit active in worship, fellowship and prayer.

The Christian life is similar to the long route marches I knew as an infantryman. In this world we are not there yet. We are not yet as Jesus is, but we are on our way to Him who is the prize of our high calling. I know this is a variant of St. Paul's metaphor in Philippians. But I am sure he does not mind. We do more marching than running. Some of us, like Pilgrim, have to plod our way to the completed citizenship of heaven.

No matter how hard or how long the route march is

for some of us, we are continuously exalted by our Lord's presence. He is with us always as He has promised: for He has exalted us to be His brothers and sisters. This is a mystery beyond adequate explanation, but not, thank God, beyond our experience.

9

Faith and Thought

The tired old arguments about reason versus faith, and science versus religion, are being buried quietly in this latter part of the twentieth century. As we have observed, all we have to do is to look around us. The English humorous magazine, *Punch*, punned the absurdity of the infantile arguments that were occurring between these poles over a hundred years ago:

What is mind?
Never matter.
What is matter?
Never mind!

We may thank today's scientists for helping us to understand that matter is not what it used to be; and that mind is a great deal more than what it was believed not to be. Dr. Arno A. Penzias, who traced the radio signal left over from the act of creation, observed in an interview in 1978: "My argument is that the data we have are exactly what I would have predicted, had I had nothing to go on but the five books of Moses, the Psalms, the Bible as a whole" (*New York Times*, 3/12/78).

Not only is matter more complex than it used to be be believed, but so is the whole process of creation. Darwin's gradualism has been replaced by the belief that creation occurred more by catastrophic explosions.

Thus, the belief in reality as cosmic progress, or matter in motion, becomes increasingly questionable, if not absurd. To think is to think about what is there, what is given. In the previous chapter, I stressed that we are responsible because we are responsive. We respond to what is there—to nature, to our fellow human beings, to God. Science is one of several disciplines. It is limited to facts. And so far it has shown its inability to deal with morality, meaning and mystery. Systems of thought which take it too seriously end up, as we have seen, in the "cul-de-sac" of rationalism, romanticism, pragmatism and despair.

What *is there* may be there for an awfully long time before someone asks why it is there, or why apples fall. Johannes Kepler (1571-1630), for example, asked the question, "Why?" because of his theological understanding of the work of the Holy Spirit. Because of his speculation, there emerged the concept of a physical power holding the heavenly bodies together. Out of this understanding developed the theory of gravity.

Similarly, Sir Isaac Newton (1642-1727), believed the physical world was the order of divine creation. Because it is, it is, therefore, capable of being understood in an orderly and reasonable way. In presenting his reason for writing his great work, *Philosophiae Naturalis Principia Mathematica*, he stated that his principles were simply a means of enabling others to believe more strongly "in a Deity." It was his faith that initiated his research. In turn, his research was offered as a means of increasing faith.

Turning closer to home, it is interesting to note that Benjamin Franklin (1706-1790) was the first to believe in the law of matter's conservation as a consequence of his belief in the conservation of souls.

Dr. Robert E.D. Clark, an organic chemist in

England, has stated in his excellent book, *Science and Christianity: A Partnership* (Pacific Press Publishing Co.), that "Without Christianity, scientific discovery on a higher level than that known to the ancient Greeks, Romans, or Chinese seems unlikely."

This thesis was upheld by the atomic scientist, Dr. Robert Oppenheimer (1904-1967), in a speech at Chicago, shortly before his death. And this subject may be read more fully in Professor Stanley Jaki's highly developed thesis in his book, *Science and Creation.*

Let us return to Dr. Clark. He has presented the case for Basic Elements of Faith in Science in eight simple propositions. These are:

1. It is essential for a scientist to believe that "there is a contrast between *truth and error.*" Without this faith in ultimate truth, and the ability to determine between true and false conclusions, science as we know it could not exist.

2. Underlying all scientific speculation is the belief "that the universe must be taken seriously." It is the biblical faith in the God who saw that His creation was good that makes such a premise possible.

3. The belief in the reasonableness of creation is a belief that "assumes that everyone in the world experiences reality in the same way." It has to be noted, I think, that this belief is more characteristic of a culture based on the Christian faith than perhaps some others which do not perceive anything unusual about individual consciousness.

4. Without a "belief in the unity of nature," which is derived from the biblical view of creation, the scientific enterprise would be highly unlikely.

5. Next is the assumption that "science will never end." Such an assumption, of course, implies an un-

ending universe. One that is identified in Christian services of worship as: "world without end."

6. The belief that the cosmos may not be constructed by scientific thought. *It is there.* By observation and experiment, it may, therefore, be possible to understand the laws by which it operates.

7. The expectation which determines the conclusion of an experiment expresses the bias, or belief, of the initiator.

8. The final belief is that "events which demand a *very long* arm of coincidence do not take place in nature."

It might also be added that the inability to provide explanations for certain phenomena does not mean they should be rejected. By this I mean there are facts and experiences which seem to be beyond the range of science's ability to explain satisfactorily, such as existence, consciousness, faith, hope, love, the atonement and so on.

We might also point to the necessity for beginning any experiment or enterprise with a great deal of humility, and continuing with the same degree of humility to the satisfactory conclusion. Indeed, many religious thinkers might learn more about this quality of humility from devoted scientists than from some of their colleagues.

As I may have indicated earlier, I am optimistic about the prospects for Christian thought in our times. God and the humanists seem to be giving the ball back to us. It is up to us, or some of us, to think more clearly and honestly as we seek to give reasons for the hope that is in us. We live in God's world, as a redeemed world, with the confidence of our hope. This hope makes all the difference in every sphere of existence whether it be spiritual, physical, economic, psychological or whatever.

Although one swallow may not make a spring, we should rejoice at every evidence of God's grace, especially when it comes, to our surprise, from those who do not wear the Christian label.

Bertrand Russell influenced me greatly during my youthful period of rationalism. In his *Human Society in Ethics and Politics*, he wrote glibly about faith as a substitute for lack of evidence, and a poor emotional substitute at that. It is interesting to recall that he turned to mathematics as the means of obtaining irrefutable evidence. His first tutor was his brother, who began by saying, "Now we start with axioms."

"What are they?" inquired the youthful Bertrand.

"Oh, they're things you've got to admit although we can't prove them."

So disturbed was young Bertrand by this remark that he exclaimed, "Why should I admit them if you can't prove them?"

His brother replied laconically, "Well, if you won't, we can't go on."

As we know, he went on through "unyielding despair" to a position which helps to integrate faith and thought by showing that reason and faith are not at opposite ends of the spectrum. They are common to both science and religion. In his essay on *Mysticism and Logic*, he concludes that intuition and reason are dependent upon each other. Insight results in beliefs which are later tested by reason, whose role is that of a harmonizer.

This conclusion is similar to that which was reached by Dr. Wilder Penfield, namely, that reason is the function of the brain, which is like a computer. Creative thought and morality belong to the activity of the mind, which is like energy or spirit.

Once again we return to the Christian view of man as

a member of two worlds, both of which are inseparably united in Him. This is the mystery of His creation. He is burdened with the ability to make decisions and to think. Decisions and thought about space, time and movement seem relatively simple. But the further the investigations initiated by them take us, the less simple they seem to be. We are often led by such investigations to doubt the simple formulas with which we began. Ultimate answers elude even the most pragmatic of formulas.

At one time the thing to do was to concentrate upon the natural order, and leave what was termed the supernatural order to God. By doing so, it would seem that the pragmatists have brought us to the point of extinction by starvation, plague, revolution, pollution, or a nuclear holocaust. The study of nature alone may well lead us to the position where we yearn for something better, something that transcends a quantitative universe.

Whether we like it or not, honest thinking cannot exclude those possibilities which exceed its range. I doubt if anyone has given a better insight into the mystery of human thought than Pascal (1623-1662) in his *Pensées*, where among other things, he shows that although we may be small and insignificant in the universe and as weak as reeds, nevertheless we are *thinking reeds*. We, alone in the universe, are aware of the universe, even as it crushes us by its physical might.

In saying this, Pascal recognizes no fine line between thought and consciousness, or reason and faith. It is my conviction that our thinking, if it is serious, leads us to the point when we cry out for revelation, which is knowledge beyond our reach, but not beyond our experience. Like St. Paul we know that we know only in part, and long to know, even as we are fully known.

Who is it that knows us fully; and who shares his knowledge with us? Indeed, who is it that has created us to ask questions, including those we cannot answer? According to the Bible, it is God who raises the first question: for it is He who initiates the dialogue of life. His invitation is a gracious one, "Come now, and let us reason together" (Isa. 1:18).

We have noted how God asks the question about ourselves by saying, "Where art thou?" To this question each one of us is made responsible for giving our own honest answer. Like Jacob, we become wrestlers with God. This is the meaning of "Israel"—one who wrestles with God (Gen. 32:24-28), whether he likes it or not. Some do it gladly, but most, reluctantly. The outstanding example of a true Israelite in our time is Aleksandr Solzhenitsyn.

Job represents those who lead upright lives, but find that life is bigger than their goodness. When Job rested his case for the defense in his trial with God, he pleaded for an answer to his problem. The answer was not given in terms of a theodicy, but in terms of God's creative power. The consequence of this answer was that Job understood God at first hand, "I have heard of thee by the hearing of the ear: but now mine eye seeth thee. Wherefore I abhor myself, and repent in dust and ashes" (Job 42:5, 6).

It was at this point of the divine/human confrontation that Job's life began anew. It was a moment of rebirth. His longing for justification was answered, not in terms of justice, but in terms of creation. The answer to Job, of course, was not completed until the Incarnation. Jesus is both the question and the answer, the *Alpha* and the *Omega*. A beautiful expression of this truth is contained in the following words of William Temple

(1628-1699), one of the great archbishops of the Church of England:

> When Reason says, "It is God who made all the world: He is, therefore, responsible; it is He who should suffer";
> We answer, "Yes, of course; He does suffer; look at the cross!"
> And when Reason cries, "If God were the loving God of whom we speak, He could not endure the misery of His children, His heart would break";
> We answer, "Yes, of course, it does break; look at the cross!"
> And when Reason exclaims, "God is infinite and ineffable; it is blasphemy to say we know Him; we cannot know Him";
> We answer, "No, not perfectly; but enough to love Him; look at the cross!"
>
> (*The Faith and Modern Thought*)

When we are asked to prove God, we need not hesitate to say we cannot. We cannot prove God the same way we can prove a simple mathematical theory. Indeed, there is so little of consequence that we may prove. I cannot, for example, prove that my wife loves me. Her love is there. What kind of dolt would I be if I did not accept it thankfully?

For the past few centuries so many people have talked about reason, knowledge and science that most people have heard very little about faith except when it is referred to in derision. I regret to say that too many radio preachers have done their best—or rather worst—to justify such criticism. In the hope of encouraging a deeper awareness of faith, I am referring to a few simple ways of thinking about it. You, undoubtedly, have already thought about it in greater depth.

Primary faith. Faith is what we are as human beings. Without it we would not begin to think or act. Some of my psychiatrist friends tell me that one form of insanity is due to a lack of faith. I know of some people who are so ill that they call me at all times of the day and night to ask me to make very simple decisions for them. Some deep fear or other obsession has controlled them so strongly that they cannot think clearly, far less make a decision. Presumably it was this sort of thing the psychiatrists were referring to. I have observed it is not a matter of intelligence: for several of my midnight callers have been postdoctoral research associates.

I can see why Jesus said, "Except ye . . . become as little children, ye shall not enter into the kingdom of heaven" (Matt. 18:3). Life begins with faith. I know of a former prisoner of war of the Japanese who had an experience of being born again. After the war he returned to England and to his former business. He went to church, and became the head of a vast company. One day he said to himself, "All I'm doing is making money. Yet, this is all I can do. But there must be something better. What? What? What have I done other than make money? I've been a prisoner-of-war. Maybe I can do something to help prisoners! What? Better find out, hadn't I?" He did his homework and found that nearly 80 percent of prisoners are recidivists (i.e., they keep returning to prison). He resigned his position, bought one of the stately homes of England, staffed it with mature Christian friends, and began the ministry of redeeming recidivists. His project went well. The percentage of recidivism among his alumni dropped to 20 percent and reversed the going rate.

The success of his method was that of taking Jesus' teaching seriously, "Except you become as a little child." My friend provided a home, foster parents, uncles, aunts, brothers and sisters that the people had never known before. In an atmosphere of trust, they learned to have trust; in an atmosphere of faith, they learned to have confidence (con-*fideo*, with faith); in an atmosphere of love, they learned to love. But they had to start at the beginning, and the associates had to learn the infinite patience of loving parents and friends.

The Home Secretary, in charge of prisons, was so impressed by the results that he commissioned my friend to initiate as many similar homes as possible. The tragedy was that he could only enlarge his activities slowly, not because of money or manors, but because of a shortage of capable people.

I mention this example as a model of primary faith. It is God's gift to everyone; but it has to be nurtured tenderly, patiently, lovingly.

Jesus knew this so well, that is why the word faith (*pistis* in Greek) was given a new meaning by Him. We should, therefore, remind ourselves of how He has made the meaning plain.

The man of perfect faith. All one has to do is to read the first three chapters of St. Mark to catch a quick glimpse of how the man of faith encouraged faith in others. Was not this why the people were amazed at the uniqueness of His teaching? "He wasn't like the teachers of the Law; instead, he taught with authority" (Mark 1:22 TEV). So unique was this authority that the very first group to recognize it as divine were the evil spirits. "I know who you are: you are God's holy messenger" (Mark 1:24 TEV). Here St. Mark is showing us how the evil spirits realized the Lord of all had come. No wonder they trembled in the very fear with which they sought to dominate others: for now "the prince of this world" was being cast out. The son of the vineyard owner was claiming His own country, and His own people. The dominion of evil was being destroyed.

Its destruction was seen in the healing miracles of Jesus. He encouraged sick folk to have faith to be whole. He imparted the power of His own faith to them. When He gave His faith to others, He gave His strength as well. So great was the need of this faith that He was often exhausted by the demands made upon Him. The only place where He could not perform a miracle was in His own home town of Nazareth. Why not? You know the answer: because there was no faith.

It is well to remember that it was of His disciples that Jesus said, "Oh, ye of little faith," and that it was a very humble and grateful father who made the prayer for all of us, "Lord, I believe; help thou mine unbelief" (Mark 9:24). The point of remembering is that our faith is inadequate because it is immature. To live in the fullness of faith is to live victoriously in the freedom of love. We know of only one man who lived in this way.

As we read the pages of the Gospels, we see how the imprisoned faith of crippled and diseased people was liberated. Such faith was not simply faith in faith, but in Jesus. The most important facet of faith was to see in Him the divine authority. As I have mentioned the first to be conscious of this power were the evil spirits. The next group was made up of outsiders such as the Syrophoenician woman and the Roman centurion. It was of this pagan soldier that Jesus said, "I have not found so great faith, no, not in Israel" (Matt. 8:10). The steps in the development of faith, from primary to mature, which I have referred to in chapter 5, are presented to us in the story of the man who had been born blind, and are worthy of expansion.

In the eighth chapter of his Gospel, John shows us how Jesus was rejected by the religious people in the

Temple in Jerusalem. So violent was their reaction to Him that they tried to stone Him. After leaving the Temple, Jesus saw the blind man. His disciples, thinking within the thought patterns of their time, asked Him who was responsible for this evidence of sin—His parents or himself? His reply literally blew their minds. He told them, "Neither." His blindness was for a purpose, namely, that the power of God might be seen working in Him. Jesus obviously had broken with the popular religious thought of His day. Illness and blindness happened in a fallen world regardless of the righteousness of the afflicted. It is to this world of blindness that Jesus has come as God's Son to do God's work.

Jesus healed the man. The miracle was beyond the comprehension of his neighbors. They, therefore, brought him to the Pharisees for an explanation. Their verdict was that Jesus was not from God because He broke the law of the Sabbath by healing on that day. In their confusion, they asked the once-blind man his opinion of his healer. It was: "He is a prophet." The miracle was denied. His parents were consulted. They confirmed that he had been born blind, but that they did not know how the miracle had occurred. Their son was called again to give evidence. His healer was identified as a sinner. Now that the experts had their say they obviously expected him to agree. He did not. He stood by his evidence: "Whether he be a sinner or no, I know not: one thing I know, that, whereas I was blind, now I see" (John 9:25).

He went on to challenge the conclusion of his inquisitors, and to state that Jesus must be of God, otherwise He could not have done what He did. This infuriated the experts. They excommunicated him. When Jesus heard of this, He sought him out and asked if he believed in the Son of God. "Who is he Lord, that I might believe in him?" was the reply of the man.

Jesus answered: "Thou hast both seen him, and it is he that talketh with thee" (John 9:37).

The man now saw Jesus with the eyes of faith. With his new understanding, he made his commitment, "Lord, I believe" (John 9:38).

We could say that primary faith needs an object outside of itself in order to understand itself. That object—or center—is not in tradition, convention, laws, dogmas, and creeds, no matter how good they may be. Once primary faith is locked into this prison, it is stunted and deformed. It has to go further. First of all, it has to go to the evidences of grace that know no boundaries. Then, to the evidence that gives sight to the blind: the Word become flesh.

I know this is true of my own experience. I saw no evidence of God in governments and their demands. I was turned off by the judgmental self-righteousness of some religious people. I saw God at work in the lives of a few faithful men. They introduced me to Jesus. My eyes were opened, and I made my commitment, "Lord, I believe." I hope, however, to refer to the theology of this experience later. At the moment it is sufficient to understand that our primary faith having been brought to maturity in Jesus, is now fulfilled in, and through, Him.

This position is true to the teaching of the New Testament. The great chapter on faith in Hebrews 11 tells us that faith is what life is all about. It is the evidence of the unseen, and inexplicable. It is observed in the history of the people of faith. Their faith pointed to Jesus who fulfilled it. In turn, those whose faith has been completed by the historic event of the Word becoming flesh, justify the faith of those who lived before this event.

In Romans, St. Paul tells us how faith operates. In chapter five, we learn we are justified by our faith in Jesus. He is our justifier: the one who stands beside us to claim us as His own. In doing so, He protects us by His righteousness. Justification results in a deep peace—the peace of reconciliation. The next stage is life in the freedom of grace. Our freedom, that is, is within the divine freedom. Earlier in Romans 1:16, 17 we are told that faith is the means of receiving right-eousness. Romans 3:25, 26 shows us that the meaning of this righteousness is displayed for all to see clearly by the sacrifice of Jesus on the cross. St. Paul goes on to tell us in Galatians that it is by faith that we both respond to this sacrifice and appropriate it for ourselves. Yet while we do, we realize that what is perfected in Jesus still has to be perfected in us. We are on the way, that is, to that end. Our present situation in the world is that we live in Christ and He in us: "I am crucified with Christ: nevertheless I live; yet not I, but Christ liveth in me: the life which I now live in the flesh I live by the faith of the Son of God, who loved me, and gave himself for me" (Gal. 2:20).

It may be helpful to go and make a brief analysis of faith's operation.

Faith as loyalty and trust. Earlier I mentioned that whatever we are as human beings, we have this capacity to give our loyalty to a cause, or a country, or an ideology, or a leader. Some will even go to the length of dying for whatever they have given their loyalty to. Although this may seem good, we have to remember we also have the ability of fixing our loyalty on the wrong standard. Millions and millions of people have died for doing this. They have followed false messiahs, hopeless causes and mad tyrants to their deaths.

I see this quality of loyalty as an aspect of primary faith. Its fulfillment we know can only come about by our obedience to Jesus' command, "Take up [your] cross, and follow me" (Matt. 16:24). Our ability to be loyal is fulfilled as trust. We could say that this is the foundation of all authentically personal life. I have noted how faith is essential for normal existence. When it does not flower as trust, the individual becomes fearful, anxious and withdrawn. A child who is not trusted soon becomes aware of the fact and exists accordingly, unless grace intervenes.

Trust is the dynamic of relationship, and the bond of friendship. It is the only way we may understand each other. Try to know another person as a thing, in the same way that we know a pound of sugar, and the other is no longer a person. I have a daughter and a son whom I love dearly. I know their height, weight, age, the color of their eyes and hair, the educational statistics from their schools and universities, and the evaluation of their work by critics. From this knowledge I have of them, I know nothing of them. As people I love and trust, I do know them. I know them as persons because they have revealed themselves to me in ways that defy analysis.

It is in trusting that we know one another, and by it we are known. This activity, I believe, is the work of the Word—the work we term "revelation." St. John, after all, has told us the Word "was in the beginning with God. . . . and without him was not anything made that was made" (John 1:2, 3).

Human existence is the nursery where we learn to trust one another by trusting our Father in heaven whose trustworthiness has been revealed in Jesus. During the period of the Old Covenant, the name for God was expressed by the Tetragrammaton transcribed YHWH. So holy was this name that the Israelites never used it, unless rarely by the High Priest; instead they used a common word, *ādōn*, meaning master or Lord. The unnameable God was named by Jesus in the Aramaic as *Abba*: the first sound a baby makes with his lips regardless of his ethnic origin. It is the response of a baby to the trusting mother or father. The relationship between God and ourselves is so intimate, Jesus is telling us, that it is like that of a parent and a baby. That is why when we pray, we say, "Our Daddy. . . ." This was the first name Jesus used to tell others of His identity, "Did you not know that I must be about my Daddy's business?" It was also the last: "Daddy, into thy hands I commit my spirit."

We have seen that it is through this perfect trust that Jesus reconciles us to our Daddy, thereby achieving at-one-ment. By this act of perfect trust, our wills are no longer alienated. This awareness, articulated in the Nicaean Creed, was the great achievement of the Council of Nicaea in 325 A.D. So complete was Jesus' trust in His *Abba* that in Him the human and the divine wills were perfectly one. That is why we believe Jesus was very man of very man, and very God of very God. He has justified our trust in His Father. The place and time where this was demonstrated was outside the walls of civilization in the time of Caesar Augustus. That demonstration, however, continues day by day.

Faith as appropriation of the past and the future. Faith is like a magic carpet: it enables us to transcend space and time. It does so because the power of transcendence is in the object of faith, namely God. St. Paul tells the Ephesians, for example, that God has initiated this faith by choosing us before we are born: "Blessed be the God and Father of our Lord Jesus Christ, who hath blessed us with all spiritual blessings in heavenly places in Christ: according as he hath chosen us in him before the foundation of the world, that we should be holy and without blame before him in love: Having predestinated us unto the adoption of children by Jesus Christ to himself" (Eph. 1:3-5). Thus, by faith we participated in the eternal, while yet existing in space and time.

In this way we appropriate God's saving acts in the past, as well as His saving acts in the future. St. Paul's letter to the Galatians explains how we are justified by faith rather than by the works of law. By this faith we are justified long, long before we are conscious of it. I know that this is hard to understand, and harder still to explain. What we might think about is that God's salvation has been worked out before it became necessary for us to accept it. When I went to university, my mother gave me a bond which she had bought before I was born. I cashed it, and paid my first year's tuition, and room and board bill. Thus, my initial university fees had been paid for long before I contemplated going to university. I am led to believe, therefore, that what is termed conversion happens in the same way. Salvation is there! By faith we appropriate it. St. Paul writes, "Even as Abraham believed God, and it was accounted to him for righteousness. Know ye therefore that they which are of faith, the same are the children of Abraham" (Gal. 3:6, 7).

In response to St. Paul we could say that faith has a long history—one that is mine as I write this in the year of our blessed Lord 1978; for my end is in my beginning.

The sacramental statement of this is, of course, the Lord's Supper. St. Paul tells us about it in 1 Corinthians 11:23-26. By participating in this sacrament, we are restating our salvation history. We are taking our place with the twelve in the Upper Room. Their faith is our faith, and our faith is their faith. We are one with them, just as they were one with Him. Did not Jesus pray that this would be the case? "Neither pray I for these alone [the disciples], but for them also which shall believe on me through their word; That they all may be one; as thou, Father, art in me, and I in thee, that they also may be one in us" (John 17:20, 21).

For a service of worship to be authentic, we gather by faith round our Lord's Table along with Peter, James, John, Andrew, Philip, Bartholomew, Matthew, Thomas, James, Thaddaeus, Simon and Judas, and all the glorious company on earth and in heaven. We are indeed one with all the saints because our center is eternal.

At the same time as we appropriate God's saving acts in the past, we appropriate those of the future. We remember that our faith is not just faith in ourselves, in the Church, in the creeds, in the sacraments, in the Bible; it is faith *in* Jesus. In this faith, we name Him Lord and God. We name Him Lord here and now because He is Lord of the beginning, of the past, of the future, of the *eschaton*. The resurrection and ascension of our Lord imply our involvement in His continuing and ultimate victory. Think of these words: "And what is the exceeding greatness of his power to us-ward who believe, according to the working of his mighty power, which he wrought in Christ, when he raised him from the dead, and set him at his own right hand in the heavenly places, far above all principality, and power, and might, and dominion, and every name that is named, not only in this world, but also in that which is to come: and hath put all things under his feet, and gave him to be the head over all things to the church, which

is his body, the fulness of him that filleth all in all"
(Eph. 1:19-23). What is this an expression of but faith
taking wings to soar? It is in this soaring that we see
how all things come from Jesus, go to Him, are for Him,
are in Him, and through Him, and by Him, who is the
Alpha and the *Omega*.

We are constantly reminded that our salvation is the
work of God. He has redeemed our past and our future.
It is already accomplished even as we exist in this
world of space and time. Let us soar again on more
words of St. Paul: "Even when we were dead in sins,
[God] hath quickened us together with Christ . . . and
hath raised us up together, and made us sit together in
heavenly places in Christ Jesus: that in the ages to
come he might show the exceeding riches of his grace
in his kindness toward us through Christ Jesus" (Eph.
2:5-7).

If you do not quite understand this teaching of St.
Paul, do not worry; no one does. Do not look upon it as
the exact measurement of eternity and the ways of God.
Instead, see it as the poetry of the heart that pours out
in exaltation as it responds to the wonder of the divine
revelation. By faith in our ascended Lord, we know the
future is secure. It is bound to be. It is in His hands.

Although it is, there are American Christians who
are scared stiff of the future, and the *eschaton*. What
is more, they regard such neurotic fear as a virtue. It
is not. What it is, is lack of faith. Knowing that the
eschaton means the last day, the day of the Lord, where
are we to place it in time? At the end of time? In the last
judgment away out there somewhere? The Jews of
Jesus' day believed that. I do not.

I believe that the day of the Lord came with Jesus.
Was not that why He said, "The time is fulfilled, and
the kingdom of God is at hand: repent ye, and believe

the gospel" (Mark 1:15). Does not this mean that the *eschaton* transcends time? If time is completed, and the kingdom has come in Jesus, then is not everyone in space and time open to the same salvation and judgment? The Word that was in the beginning, and the Word that is at the end, is the same Word. This same Word is the Word we know in the flesh, and through the flesh, and His name is Jesus.

The Gospel according to the beloved John is a glorious expression of our faith in Jesus through whom we have eternal life. This eternal life transcends space and time, otherwise it would not be worthy of the name eternal. Our faith in Jesus leads us through the barrier of time into the eternal openness. The six great I AM declarations of Jesus are the affirmations of this truth. The one I shall mention is in John 11:25, 26. Martha, along with Nicodemus and other Pharisees, believed that the *eschaton* was away out yonder in distant time; that is why she said to Jesus: "I know that [Lazarus] shall rise again in the resurrection at the last day." Jesus' reply is extremely well known:

I am the resurrection, and the life:
he that believeth in me,
though he were dead,
yet shall he live:
And whosoever liveth and believeth in me
shall never die.
Believest thou this?

Again, we are confronted with the mystery of salvation: by faith we live on the frontiers of this world, and the kingdom of God. Our fellowship is not with a dead Christ, but with the living one. Even within our dying bodies, we have eternal life. We are alive now!

St. John's letters make this perfectly clear, particularly in 1 John 4:17. "Herein is our love made perfect, that we may have boldness in the day of judgment: because as he is, so are we in this world."

Those trembling Christians I referred to are fearful of the judgment that has already come. They ask, "What should we do until Jesus returns?" Surely we know!

We are to be faithful, which means enduring in our faith. Indeed, St. Paul tells us in Romans 5:4 that such endurance is the evidence of our hope: for by such endurance, we are approved of God. Along with our enduring faith, goes our enduring love. Presumably someone had asked Jesus what He should do until the Son of man came in His glory: for Jesus' reply was to feed the hungry, satisfy the thirsty, befriend the stranger, clothe the naked, attend to the sick and visit the prisoners. Read all about it in the last parable (Matt. 25:31-46).

Thus, the note sounded by the Christian faith is a high and victorious one. It is the evidence of God's *Yes* to us.

Faith as Yes! When we looked at the biblical teaching about man and sin, we saw that the fallen condition of the human race is one in which all of us have said *NO* to God in our own original way. This seems to be about the only original thing that we do in our godless existence. This human *NO* is made brilliantly clear in the first chapter of the Letter to the Romans. This *NO* is the illusion of pride, "professing themselves to be wise, they became fools" (Rom. 1:22). Despite this negative attitude, God never stops calling us to be His kinsfolk. Our *yes* to Him is the response of our faith, and this becomes our *no* to the dominion of the prince of this world.

The more we learn to say *yes*, the easier does it become to say *no*. The cross is the measure of the *no*. This was, and is, mankind's refusal to accept the truth about itself, and its alienation from God and His purpose.

All of us know what it means to be subject to the tyranny of the human *no*. No, you cannot do this; no, you cannot do that; no, you cannot live except as the law admonishes you; no, you cannot be free except as we permit it; no, you must not regard human beings as important; no, you cannot live at peace, you must prepare for war; no, you must not accept other human beings as equal; no, you must not regard children as human beings on a par with us superior adults; no, no, no!

My own experience of the kingdom of negation and futility was that I had so many *noes* crammed down my throat that I suffered from an acute case of spiritual indigestion.

I experienced the lordship of Jesus as a big *YES*. Strangely enough I found more *yeses* than *noes* in the Church, although I have so often criticized her for not having enough *yeses*.

The gospel is good news—news that affirms our daily existence in the most positive of ways. That is why we find St. Paul writing so positively to the negative Christians at Corinth to tell them that Jesus is God's "Yes"; for it is he who is the "Yes" to all of God's promises (2 Cor. 1:20).

I find that when I have to visit a secular bureaucracy for some reason or other, all I come away with is a pocketful of *noes*. When I pray, or when I worship in the fellowship of Christ's brethren, my empty pocket is filled with *yeses*. And of course this is as it should be: for God has said a loud and joyful *Yes* to us in Jesus our Lord. By this *Yes* our negated lives are transformed into creative power.

Faith as miraculous. I would hate to define a miracle. For me it means a happening outside the secular order of things, an occurrence, however, that is according to God's purpose for His people. It is the same as a moment of grace, or any moment that is beyond the limitations of human reason and its systems.

Wherever Jesus was, in the days of His flesh, miracles happened. He never made a big thing of it, however. His miracles were for particular individuals at particular times, according to their particular needs. Apart from the feeding of the four and the five thousand, I do not recall an incident of mass miracles. On the contrary, Jesus tried to keep His miracles as secret as possible. The record of His temptations is that He chose not to be known as a miracle worker.

At one time theologians used the element of the miraculous as a proof of Jesus' divinity. Jesus never did. It was sufficient that people should believe in Him for His own sake. More important than the miracles are His teachings, and His statements of authority which were introduced by the amen of God—"Truly, truly, I say unto you" and His encounters with people; and His questions, ". . . but who do you say that I am?"; and His death; and His resurrection.

Miracles happened wherever He was. This did not prove to the religious people of His time that He was the Son of God. On the contrary, it only proved to them that He was in the pay of Beelzebub. When many Jews became Christians, the rabbis of their time tried to assert that His miracles, even the raising of Lazarus, were the work of the devil as their *apologia* against Christianity.

The more His disciples learned to trust Jesus, the more they were able to do miracles as well. What was required was faith in God, and in the righteousness of

His rule. So far as I can judge, it was faith in Jesus that released the creative power that made miracles happen.

Having said this, I am not so sure I can say much more. I do not equate miracles with magic. I equate them, however, with the creative power God makes available to us. When I was a prisoner of war in Thailand, we had no bread, medicines,·or money. Devout Christians prayed for these needs. No matter how hard they prayed, pennies and bread did not drop from heaven. And yet what I believe to be miracles happened whenever men turned to Jesus as Lord and believed in one another. Such miracles were part of the fabric of our existence.

Our medical doctors encouraged faith healing by encouraging men to have faith. When our camp was transformed from a death camp to a community of faith, many men became healers according to their abilities. One man had agonized over his suffering comrades who had their limbs cut off with a carpenter's saw without benefit of an anaesthetic. His agony was that of love. He used it creatively. With the help of two botanists, he discovered certain alkali-producing plants in the jungle which he synthesized to produce an effective local anaesthetic. It was his faith that initiated the thinking and the experiments that made that miracle happen.

Another similar one was the creation of medicine from living bacteria. So expert did he become in this field that he went on to become one of England's leading biochemists. This, too, was a miracle, for his education before the war had terminated at the ninth-grade level.

Some of my friends developed a blood transfusion system. They grabbed any healthy looking prisoner and dragged him to the side of a sick man so they could siphon off a pint of blood. Few of us were healthy enough to supply two. By the sharing of our blood, we kept each other alive. For those of us who survived, it seemed miraculous.

My own efforts were very minor. I became a masseur; I am glad to report that because of this, paralyzed men walked. I do not think this happened as a consequence of my expertise. Rather it was because I touched "diseased" men with the touch of love and communicated to them a little of my faith. For those who walked again, it seemed miraculous enough.

In the same way, we created a university, a symphony orchestra, artificial legs, Christmas puddings and other things. All of them grew out of what was at hand like the spittle and clay Jesus used to heal blindness.

Perhaps the biggest miracle of all in those days was the miracle of faith. This miracle, I rejoice to report, still occurs. It is such faith, rather than the method, that creates miracles, usually in the most practical of ways. I think the following story illustrates my point.

A woman heard her neighbor's husband had become a Christian, and her neighbor had been converted with him. She decided to have the facts for herself, so she asked the neighbor if she believed all "this Jesus stuff." Her neighbor admitted that she did. The woman felt she was losing her position as skeptic too quickly so she pulled out her trump card: "But you don't believe in miracles, do you? Surely you can't be so far gone as that? All that stuff about turning water into wine?"

To her astonishment, her neighbor answered that she did believe in such miracles. "You remember what Tom was like? He was aye drinking. All his pay went to the pubkeeper on a Saturday night. You'll remember as well that I had to sell our furniture to pay our bills.

Now look around you! If that is not a miracle, I don't know what is. Since Tom turned to Jesus, Jesus has turned whiskey into furniture."

Where there is faith, miracles happen. Perhaps not in our way. That should not worry us. What matters is that it should be in God's way. What better place is there, by the way, for miracles to happen, according to the needs of our time, than on university campuses? All that is required is people of faith. This was the point made by St. Paul to the Galatians when he told them: "He therefore that ministereth to you the Spirit, and worketh miracles among you, doeth he it by the works of the law, or by the hearing of faith?" (Gal. 3:5). It is this faith that makes all the difference.

Faith as intensification of consciousness

Nowhere should the evidence of faith be seen more clearly than in our personal lives. To be in the Spirit is to bear the fruits of the Spirit. This harvest occurs more slowly than we would like. Yet it happens! No matter how slowly, it results in an intensification of consciousness. Increasingly we know who we are, because we know whose we are. As we become more aware of Jesus as Lord we become more aware of ourselves, our neighbors, and the neighborhood around us. With the eyes of faith we see what was once hidden. We perceive the divine mystery behind everything. We understand our existence in depth and height. Our thoughts take wings to soar like the eagle. In her hymn, Harriet Beecher Stowe expresses something of this new and unique consciousness in these words:

Fairer than morning, lovelier than daylight,
Dawns the sweet consciousness I am with Thee.

When our self-consciousness is transformed into

214

Christ-consciousness, we are in the condition that St. Paul writes about as, "I am crucified with Christ: nevertheless I live; yet not I, but Christ liveth in me" (Gal. 2:20). As we die the many deaths necessary for being in Christ, we are liberated to be more aware of God's will and purpose for us. Because the center of existence is no longer within ourselves, we have the advantage of viewing life from the highest of perspectives. At sea level we have a very limited horizon. On the top of Mount Everest, on a clear day, the horizon is relatively limitless.

The quality of this consciousness identifies us increasingly as Christ's kinsmen. We become His letters, known and read by all men. Because I have seen the difference this new consciousness makes in the lives of others, I have been pointed to Jesus as its initiator. Such an experience I believe to be the activity of the Holy Spirit, the living Word.

The quality of this consciousness has marked Christians throughout the centuries, and marked them as different from Romans, or Hindus, or Moslems, or Communists, or Nazis, or Humanists. I have been intrigued by St. Luke's record of Paul's missionary journeys, particularly the one that took him to his imprisonment in Rome. Nothing seemed to frighten him. Although he was a prisoner, he commanded his guards. In the shipwreck he took over from the ship's captain, and put everyone at ease. As a shipwrecked prisoner on Melita, the islanders came to mistake him for a god. In Rome, where he was a prisoner for two years, he preached the kingdom of God to all who would hear him, including his prison guards.

We see this same kind of personal quality in Solzhenitsyn. His way to Christ was through imprisonment and suffering. It was in captivity that he found his freedom. Such is the intensity of his consciousness that some people feel threatened by it. Shortly after his address to the graduating class of 1978 at Harvard, I heard a professor of politics criticize him for "bringing religion into it." The professor felt this was something he had no right to do, because it made others feel uncomfortable. Such a criticism is by no means uncommon.

Soren Kierkegaard has referred to the Christian faith as "that happy passion." This means much the same as Pascal's gamble. The words "passion" and "gamble" indicate the intensity of faith's involvement. It results in a particular way of life, in independency of thought, heroism of action, stubbornness of will, dedication to truth, and antagonism to evil. Jesus intended nothing less. He would not recruit half-hearted followers. He tells us that our *yes* is to be *yes*, and our *no*, *no*. To call Him Lord means doing what He commands regardless of one's loss of popularity.

One of the greatest lacks in every field of endeavor today is men and women of integrity willing to bet their lives on the triumph of righteousness. When apathy is the norm, those who burn with the moral passion of the Christian faith stick out like sore thumbs, and thereby embarrass the upholders of the status quo.

I believe it was this intensity of consciousness that was seen by the world in the post-Pentecost Church. It was for this reason that many of the saints were martyred. It was for this same reason, however, that many joined the ranks of the Church. They had seen the evidence for Jesus in the life style of His kinsfolk. They had also seen that the community of faith lived in a way that was greatly different from the ways of Caesars and their governments. It was the way of life.

Faith and reason. The early Christians were said by T.R. Glover to have outlived, out-died, out-loved and out-thought the pagans of their day. Men of humble educational background took on intellectual giants and out-thought them. This out-thinking did not happen in a vacuum. It happened first of all in fellowship. New Christians were nurtured by mature ones. They were encouraged to share in the intensity of consciousness the Holy Spirit created. Through loving, supporting, friendly fellowship, they were introduced to Jesus so that their commitment to Him as Lord became stronger, deeper and wider. The Letter to the Hebrews seems to have been written for this purpose. The writer was encouraging a community, of which he once had been a leader, not to be afraid, not to hold back. As kinsmen of Christ they were to follow Him and go on to maturity. They could not do so if they wasted their time and their reason arguing about the exactness of doctrines (Heb. 6).

Most of St. Paul's letters would not have been written if the young churches had been mature enough to give primacy to fellowship for Jesus' sake. Thus, we find St. Paul telling the Roman church, ". . . to be likeminded one toward another according to Christ Jesus" (Rom. 15:5). That is, as Christians they are to follow the example of their Lord. In doing so, they will find harmony of will and thought. The primary witness of the Church is not to itself, but to its Lord; therefore, worship was the centering, or harmonizing, point of attention.

The grateful worship of the fellowship created the atmosphere for learning about the life, teachings and work of their Lord. This was done through preaching and teaching. We have seen how Stephen articulated the early church's understanding of history through his martyr sermon, which suggests it was known and understood by the Church as a whole as part of its mind. We have also seen how St. Peter articulated the essential proclamation (*kērugma*) of the Church. The points of this were probably discussed at length during the teaching sessions of the new Christians.

We may catch a glimpse of this educational method through the record of Saul's conversion. For three days he waited in Damascus until Ananias came to him, laid hands on him, restored his sight, and baptized him. After that, brother Saul spent a number of days—we do not know how many—with the disciples of the Damascus church who, presumably, instructed him in the *kērugma*. They did it so well that Saul, become Paul, went to the synagogues to preach Christ as the Son of God. In his Galatian account of his conversion, he tells us of how he had been devoted to the Jewish religion to the extent that he had become an expert in the tradition. Because his conversion had been the consequence of revelation, he had chosen not to go to anyone for further instruction. Instead he went to Arabia. What he did there we do not know. We may presume, however, that his time was spent in thinking and reflecting upon his experience. After his return to Damascus he became known among the brethren as ". . . he which persecuted us in times past now preached the faith which once he destroyed" (Gal. 1:23).

Anyone who studies St. Paul's letters in depth knows that he or she is grappling with a brilliant mind. So well had he thought out the reasons for his faith that he could take on, in discussion, the best intellects of the Jewish and pagan worlds. He has been criticized for being too intellectual in his address to the Athenians on Mars Hills. This criticism is usually based on the presumption that his mission was a failure. The evidence of Acts 17 does not support this bias. Although there is no evidence of mass conversions, we are told that "certain men clave unto him, and believed: among the which was Dionysius the Areopagite, and a woman named Damaris, and others with them" (Acts 17:34). Dionysius was a judge of the Athenian supreme court. Damaris was presumably a leader in the area. The point is that Paul's intellect and knowledge were at the command of the Holy Spirit. As a consequence, a group of intellectuals were brought to the point of conviction, repentance and conversion.

St. Paul could argue with the best of the humanists, but his arguments were never based on their basic faith in themselves and their reason. It is this prideful faith that he classifies as "the wisdom of the wise." Faith without revelation is dead.

It is revelation that initiates reason, which in turn, is essential to faith. I have never been able to separate them, nor to discern the dividing line between them. The character of the Christian faith, as I know it, is that it inspires and illuminates thought. Referring to my prison camp experience, I find it both inspiring and illuminating that starving men were motivated by their faith in Jesus to create an orchestra, a theater, a hospital and a university, as well as a church.

The jungle university of Chungkai had no charter, no board of trustees, no government grants, no laboratories and no administrative buildings. All it had was people who were motivated by their faith to think; and, in thinking, to think about the nature of the world, and of man and of God.

Faith and thought belong together. The object of faith determines the quality of the thinking. In the past, the Christian faith inspired great thinkers. They left behind an intellectual treasure house which has almost been used up. That is why the intellectual challenge to Christians today is as great as it was to the Church in the first three hundred years of its existence. But where are the equivalents in the United States today?

For me the Christian position regarding faith and thought is summed up in this sentence of Emil Brunner, the Swiss preacher/teacher:

Faith is reason subject to the rule of God. (*Man in Revolt*, p. 483)

We could say that the record of human thought shows it is basically a search for the reality which transcends measurements and appearances. It is a search for the metaphysical foundation of experience and all that is. Paul Tillich is not far off the mark when he speaks of faith as being grasped by the power of being. What is this but the divine tap on the shoulder that causes us to turn around in wonder?

As citizens of the two cities, we exist in the paradox of time and eternity, space and infinity, evil and good, illusion and truth, selfishness and love, man and God, the particular and the universal. Thus, "reason subject to the rule of God" is the synthesizer or harmonizer of the paradox.

The question I have to ask myself is: Why then are not people more religious and more thoughtful? The answer has already been given. We choose to limit our existence to one side of the paradox, such as space, time, matter or rational process, in our attempts to avoid the divine/human confrontation. Days of wine and roses are usually days of apathy and complacency. High religion and great thinking seem to coexist with days of crises and conflict. The year 1955 was the year when church membership peaked in this country. What peaked along with it was the cult of success and wishful thinking: the cult of wine and roses in which God was worshiped for what we can coax out of Him as a super Santa Claus.

Whether I like it or not, I can only conclude that "many are called but few are chosen" to be God-wrestlers: to respond wholeheartedly, that is, to the tap on the shoulder.

According to my experience as a Christian, to think as one means being within the mind of Christ. This is a quality of thought and living into which we grow day by day, experience by experience, thought by thought.

The *kērugma* I wrote of earlier is the hat peg of revelation and consciousness. The thinking of early Christians was centered upon the revelation of the Word become flesh. A brief summing up of the *kērugma* is as follows:

1. By the fulfillment of ancient prophecies, Jesus initiated the new age of the new creation in His own person.

2. He was of the household of David, a descendant, that is, of the greatest king of Israel on whom the Israelites pinned their hope.

3. He was executed as the Scriptures foretold according to the divine purpose.

4. He was buried.

5. In accordance with the Scriptures, He was raised by God on the third day.

6. He reigns at the right hand of the Father, in the place of ultimate authority, as the exalted Son of God, Lord of the living and the dead.

7. He will come again at the end of history, as both judge and Savior.

8. He calls us to repentance and the life of victorious cross-bearing and sharing.

At this point, I think it timely to express my gratitude

to the English New Testament scholar, C.H. Dodd, for his analysis of the *kērugma*. For me it helped to give logical form to my thinking on the experience of revelation.

Christian thought is centered upon the man Jesus. This is the hard fact which opens our minds to think imaginatively about all other hard facts. Along with the first disciples, we begin by thinking about this executed man. He was flesh and blood and bone, yet more than that. It was this quality of *more than that* which inspired the great confession of faith, "My lord, and my God." On this evidence, slight though it may seem, they pledged themselves to Him in much the same way that a wife will pledge herself to her husband—for good and for life. If they had not done this, we would not have known of Him.

What they saw in Him was the Word become flesh, "full of grace and truth as the only begotten of the Father." His Word then became flesh in His disciples, and then in the flesh of the disciples of the disciples.

What we are saying is: God encounters us in the flesh at our fleshly level.

The Word of the Incarnation is, thus, the *Word of Invitation*. It is not that we are like God so much as it is that God is like us. I think this is what Robert Browning is saying in his poem, "Saul":

> O Saul, it shall be
> A Face like my face that receives thee;
>   a man like to me,
> Thou shalt love and be loved by, forever:
>   a Hand like this hand
> Shall throw open the gate of new life to thee!
>   See the Christ stand! (XVIII)

And again,

'Tis the weakness in strength that I cry for!
my flesh that I seek
In the Godhead!

The Word of invitation is the *Word of welcome.* I confess
I am not a good, pious man. I am one who, in the crab-
biness of his personality, will respond to nothing positively except a smile and a welcome. I have found
myself, however, saying, "Yes," to the *Word of welcome*:
to the laboring man who says: "Come unto me all ye
that labor and are heavy laden"; for like many others I
have labored and known the exhaustion of labor.

When World War II ended, the group of ex-prisoners
I was with was flown to Rangoon. There we were
welcomed by a group of elderly ladies who served us
tea and sandwiches in a welcoming marquee. While I
was gulping my second gallon of tea and gobbling my
umpteenth sandwich, I noticed two GIs standing by
a table, not eating and swilling tea like myself, but
weeping. Strong men they were! Professional soldiers.
Tough fighters over seven years of action on the North-
western Frontier of India, then the action of World
War II, and then three and one-half years of harsh
captivity. And they were weeping! Cruelty, hardship,
suffering they could bear. But a kind welcome? It
touched their hearts.

I dare to mention this incident because I see it as a
model of the twentieth century. A century of holocausts, extermination camps, Gulag Archipelagos and
nuclear stockpiles. Yet in the midst of this godless
reality is the reality of the incarnated Word; God with
a smile, welcoming us: *Come unto me!*

This *welcoming Word* by its action is the *interpretive
Word.* He integrates our thinking so that we understand in part the power of the divine grace at work

within us. Thus, I may know myself not in terms of Sartre's *Nausea*, but in terms of the divine love. Now I know whose I am. I know my neighbor, for he or she is one with me in the family of many sisters and brothers, of whom Jesus is the eldest, or first-born. I know the world around me. It is not condemned. It is loved, and therefore, hopeful.

As Christians we have the confidence that God has interpreted our humanness for us: Yes, and also for himself. He knows and remembers us:

> And didst Thou take to heaven a human brow?
> Dost plead with man's voice by the marvellous sea?
> Art thou his kinsman now?

The activity of the living Word gives us our identity, and therefore, the ability to think in wonder, love and praise. Without the identity given to us by our Father's love, we would lack the ability to think creatively and personally. We would be processed computers. C.S. Lewis has warned us of this horrible possibility in his *That Hideous Strength*. This novel is a prophecy of what happens when reason is isolated from revelation. I think that a considerable number of people are aware of this possibility. It is up to Christian thinkers to think through their faith in order to help them both understand their predicament, and to have hope through God's revelation in Jesus. To do this takes a great deal of faith. We know only in part. Our intellects are limited. Our hope is in God. That is why we pray daily, "Lord, I believe; help thou mine unbelief" (Mark 9:24).

What we have to face is: what we believe is what we think about. It is seldom, if ever, that we think without believing first of all what we are thinking. I have tried to show that humanism is the faith that initiates the thought style that in turn initiates a life style that is one-dimensional. I hope I have indicated that the faith we term Christian is more original, more creative and more hopeful. And because of this, it is more thoughtful.

10

Education for Maturity

It is a time to grow up.

This is true of countries and civilizations as much as it is of individuals. Individual responsibility implies corporate responsibility. Both belong together. The Church as Christ's Body is the model which helps us to understand our mutual obligations and privileges.

I have expressed my conviction that the U.S.A. and Western civilization are reaching—if they have not done so already—the *eschaton*-point: the end point, which is also the point of no return. The religion of humanism has reinforced "man's inhumanity to man." Its disregard of mutual responsibility has left the field open for the reinforcement of irresponsibly destructive acts such as rape, murder and torture. The daily news is evidence of that negative freedom which is centered upon the self and its illusions. One of the prevailing fantasies which I presume to be an indication of the *eschaton*-point is that of sexual indulgence, which has increased enormously in recent years. It is generally regarded as good. Presumably it is evidence of the new freedom made possible by the influence of the humanist faith.

Prevailing statistics indicate that a large percentage of the population is involved in sexually organic functions at an early age. Recognizing this as good, or at least acceptable, schools and colleges provide "sex counseling" which is aimed at promoting greater sexual efficiency.

The attempts to liberate the repressed libido appear to have had destructive consequences. One news item reported that a twelve-year-old boy put his sexual counseling into practice by raping a four-year-old girl. Another news report tells of a twelve-year-old and a thirteen-year-old who broke into the flat of a seventy-three-year-old woman to rob, beat and rape her. They then stole her keys, kept her in a state of fear, and returned regularly to repeat their acts.

After the rape of a young girl in California by four youths, who were afterwards arrested, the mother of the victim brought charges against a TV company for being responsible. The reason for this charge was that the youths had admitted seeing a movie on TV which depicted a simulated rape in a girls' reformatory. The TV company argued that the charge should be dropped because it violated its right of free communication under the First Amendment.

I think it is difficult to prove that the movie in question was solely responsible for the violence of the youths; nevertheless, it seems to me that a responsible company would be likely to reexamine its policies in order to avoid programs which might contribute to the delinquency of minors. To argue on the basis of the First Amendment, according to its original purpose, is surely to argue for the free exercise of responsible communication. The basis of the company's decision to use questionable material was, in my judgment, the simple decision to make money as easily as possible.

The basic presumption of criminal law is that adults are presumed to intend the consequences of their actions. This is a presumption which takes sin, and the nature of man, seriously. When it is no longer a working premise, we are at the *eschaton*-point.

I mention this matter of erotic fantasy merely as a tiny example of looking around us. From here one could go on to analyze the moral collapse of our cities; the cynicism of international conglomerates; the tyranny of petty bureaucracy; and the brutal treatment of children by immature parents.

A *civilization under judgment*

The attitude of the Old Testament was that all judgment was of God. On this basis, Amos thundered at the children of Israel: "I will punish you for all your iniquities" (Amos 3:2), and Isaiah, referring to a more general judgment: "He shall judge among the nations" (Isa. 2:4). We are to see this judgment, however, in terms of the consequences of the actions of governments and their people.

According to the belief in progress, with its accompanying optimism about science and technology, the twentieth century might have been well up the evolutionary escalator on the way to perfection, yet the killing rate of people due to World Wars I and II, the Russian Revolution and the subsequent purges, the Spanish Civil War, Korea, Vietnam, the Middle East, prisons and concentration camps, is the highest of any century, and perhaps higher than the sum of the people killed in previous centuries.

Who dares forget that we have achieved in this century the potential for the ultimate kill rate? If conventional bombs could create five storms similar to those of Dresden, think how effectively a nuclear bombardment could burn up the life-producing oxygen of our planet. Nuclear energy is common in the cosmos; oxygen is rare—so rare that it could easily be destroyed to leave planet earth as another dead moon.

The reality of this *eschaton*-point is engraved in the unconscious minds of young people today. Often, when I am counseling students at a crisis time in their lives, this deep fear comes to the surface. It is a source of despair.

Nuclear weaponry, however, as the ultimate "Stop" sign is not reserved for the last big bang. Its effects are with us, and increasing yearly. The hot waste from nuclear projects, even of the most pacific nature, result in cancer-creating pollutants. Soon we may run out of storage space and fulfill T.S. Eliot's prophecy contained in his poem, "Hollow Men":

> This is the way the world ends
> This is the way the world ends
> This is the way the world ends
> Not with a bang but a whimper.

I do not think I need enlarge on this theme of the *eschaton*-point. You read of it daily. The pride of our humanist culture has brought us all to judgment. What do we do in the judgment?

We are probably living in the interim period described in the Book of Revelation:

> And when he had opened the seventh seal, there was silence in heaven about the space of half an hour. (Rev. 8:1)

> What do we do in the space of this half an hour?
> Weep in despair?
> Grow up quickly?

The challenge of judgment to the Church

We are reminded constantly that the Church has a body of flesh. It is subject, therefore, to the weakness,

230

pain and agony of its humanity. I think there are at least three ways in which we may act during the last half an hour.

1. As Christians, we may withdraw into the isolation of self-righteous anger. In doing this, we may nurse our "wrath to keep it warm." We could heat it up to the extent of attempting to destroy evil in the form of evildoers. The Inquisition tried to do this. And so have many religious groups. It was my experience of one of them in my student days that turned me against Christianity. This group was angry with everyone who was not like itself. When its members prayed, they shouted in anger at God to tell Him that He had to punish the sinner and that right speedily. When they talked, they talked in anger. They were against everything, and for nothing. I liked dancing, lassies, a good song and an occasional pint of beer. All of this was *verboten*, so I hastily fled the group's presence. Very honestly, I had concluded that if Christianity is not in favor of life, beauty, joy, people, love and goodness, then it is not for me.

I have noticed these days that some new Christians are so horrified by the obvious evils of society that they withdraw for solace into islands of isolation in the mistaken assumption that physical separation from the world is holiness. This "holiness" is characterized by a hatred of the world as it is, and by a severe judgmental attitude toward those who do not share the same view. At bottom there seems to be a deep insecurity and fear. Such is the quality of the basic anger of such groups that if they had the power and the means of implementing it, they would clean up the sins of the world by destroying the perpetrators of evil.

There is a Greek myth which describes this situation. It is the myth of Herakles (Hercules). He was a hero, seeking to be a demi-god, who undertook the task of purging evil from the world. After accomplishing this enormous task, he returned to his native town of Thebes. To his dismay, he was met by several youths disporting themselves in an unseemly manner. He was so angered by this display that he drew his sword and killed them. He then continued his triumphal entry to the cheers of the citizens. When he arrived at his mansion, he was met by a weeping wife. Rather than smiling over his victories, she was lamenting the fate of his victims. The youths killed by the gates were her sons, who had gone to welcome their father.

This quality of self-righteous anger is common to all of us. How horrible it is when it is sanctioned by immature Christians in the name of holiness.

2. As Christians we may try to sanctify apathy and call it righteousness. That is, we declare that the world is so evil that we can do nothing about it. The best we can do is to spend the half an hour of divine silence in worrying about our own souls and their salvation. I was told by an advocate of this position that I was too worldly. I cared too much for people and their problems instead of concentrating upon the condition of my soul in the light of the coming judgment. The person then went on to tell me I had to turn my back on the world because God was concerned only with our souls. Salvation was purely spiritual.

I thanked the person for his obvious concern and told him that while I was spirit, I was also flesh. So far I had not been able to communicate as a pure spirit with any other pure spirit. The fellowship I knew with Christian sisters and brothers was in the flesh as well as in the spirit. The spirit within them, and within me, depended upon the flesh as a means of communication. Indeed, the laying on of hands is a fleshly act which assures us of the presence and power of the Holy Spirit.

What is more, when a brother or sister is hungry, I feed him or her. When I see a piece of garbage polluting the countryside, I do my best to clean it up. I see this as a consequence of my faith in Jesus as Lord. The more I trust Him the more I care about the world, and the people He died for. He did not withdraw from the world to join the Essenes as an ascetic. He spent so much time in the marketplace that He was accused of being a glutton and a drunkard. And what more worldly way of dying was there than as a revolutionary?

3. The third way is the way of faithfulness. In the half an hour, we must certainly put our house in order much in the same way we do in the half hour before a hurricane strikes. This is part of our faithfulness. It is taking care of whatever our Lord gives us to do.

Perhaps the best picture we may think of is contained in the parable of the wheat and the weeds (Matt. 13:24-30). It was addressed to the disciples at a time when they seemed to be angered by the frustration of their expectations. If Jesus were indeed the Messiah, why did He not inaugurate His kingly rule?

We know that the disciples were extremely annoyed by those who did not conform to their standards. They were angry when a group of young mothers tried to break through the crowds to have their babies blessed by Jesus. They were resentful when the Canaanite woman dared to attract Jesus' attention. Remember how up-tight they were when they saw an outsider cast out demons in Jesus' name? Think of the time when they wanted to burn down the Samaritan village when the villagers lost interest in Jesus because of His obvious intention to go to Jerusalem and execution?

Most of the disciples, it seems, were tempted to join the first group I have referred to. Jesus' answer was the story of the good farmer. He sowed his fields with the best seed. One day his field hands came to tell him that his crops had been spoiled. They were shot through with a weed that looked like wheat—*zizania*. The farmer was asked if the cheat-wheat should be pulled up. *No*, said the farmer, although he knew that an enemy had spoiled his crop. Nothing was to be gained from an angry attack upon the phony wheat. The best thing to do was to let the real thing and the evil thing grow together, enjoying the same sun and nutrition until harvest time. Then they could be separated. The real wheat would endure, and the false would be burned.

What is this story if it is not about the realism of faith? The God who sends the rain on the just and the unjust alike knows what He is doing. The judgment is His, not ours. We are called upon to be faithful like the good farmer. The "half an hour" is God's time (*kairos*), not our time. The moment of judgment is in His *kairos*.

Yes, the *eschaton*-point is apparent. It was in the days of the first disciples. They knew they were existing in "the space of half an hour." In this space, they were to endure, that is, to hold fast to the faith that was theirs, and leave the judgment to God.

We may forget at times that Pentecost occurred in the *kairos* of God. Through it, or because of it, both salvation and judgment were evident. "It shall come to pass," St. Peter tells us, "that whosoever shall call on the name of the Lord shall be saved" (Acts 2:21). Because of Pentecost, the disciples did not withdraw from the world in apathy or anger, but faced it with the good news of liberation and hope. Tune your hearts to hear the ringing quality of this announcement by Peter: "Ye men of Israel hear these words" (Acts 2:22).

Is not this the very same thing that the Church has to

do and say today in "the half an hour" of time that is ours? "People of the world, hear this! Hear the good news and rejoice!"

It takes those who are mature in their faith to speak and live in this way. Let us look, therefore, at what it means to grow up in the faith.

Growing up

Our physical growth happens quickly. Between the ages of nineteen and twenty-three, we reach the physical point of maturity. After that it is downhill all the way: varicose veins, obesity, tummy ulcers, heart trouble and all the rest of the ills that flesh is heir to. Sad, is it not? But true. Although true, not hopeless.

Intellectually, we mature more slowly. Five years of home influence, twelve years of school, four years of college, four to eight years of graduate or professional school, and that is it. By the time we are thirty, we should be reasonably intellectual if we try hard enough.

Maturing in the faith is another matter. When do we mature? Never, so far as my experience is concerned. At eighty or ninety we are still infants spiritually.

We are born of the flesh, subject to the controls of our genes and environment, yet possessing the potential of transcending them, because we are created in the image of God. We have the potential, in our freedom, of growing with Him or going away from Him into the shadows of despair and death. We are born as individuals, but we become kinsmen of Christ by the adoption of the spirit. This is what happens when we are reborn. It is our experience of life-giving power of grace. When we are born again we are only at the beginning, not at the end, of the spiritual life. We are then nurtured as children in the household of faith. For some of us there is a great deal of growing up to be done before we are

235

able to digest the strong meat that is provided for those of mature spirit (Heb. 5:14; 1 Cor. 3:2).

Senator Mark Hatfield reminded me of this when he spoke in the Princeton University Chapel on the last Thursday of September, 1977. He criticized the *born-again* movement, which was receiving a lot of publicity at that time. He did so not because he disbelieved, but because he believed so strongly in the authenticity of being born again. His criticism was based on the fact that the popular movement was more the product of American culture than evidence of the kingdom of God.

He pointed out that the second birth is the action of grace. This, in turn, means "a dramatically transformed stance toward all life." This stance is one which is characterized by a transformation:

from domination to servanthood,
from materialistic values to spiritual realities,
from retribution to forgiveness,
from violence to long-suffering love,
from competition to cooperation,
from oppression to justice and liberation,
from the security of wealth to a costly compassion
   for the poor.

Such a transformation is the same as that required of us by the Sermon on the Mount. The inward or spiritual life is, as we have noted, the dynamic of all authentically moral action. What we will, we do! What we say with our lives is often clearer than what we say with our lips.

Let us remember once more that to be born again means the birth of the spirit, and the beginning of a new life with a new mind and a new style of life. It is a starting point: not a terminus. This new beginning occurs in old bodies. All of our experiences before conversion leave their mark on us. Some of us bear the wounds of hard and dangerous living, and some of the marks of the soft life and the privileged environment. The change that takes place in these mortal bodies is that they become the temples of the Holy Spirit, the fleshly homes, that is, of His activity.

To grow up is to mature in the spirit under the tutelage of the Holy Spirit. This growing up occurs within the Church, the Body of Christ, the divine/human fellowship. As our Lord taught His disciples in the days of His flesh, so the Holy Spirit teaches us today in the days of our flesh, and the sphere of His teaching activity is the Church.

The final discourses of Jesus recorded by St. John in the thirteenth to the seventeenth chapters take us to the heart of the spiritual life. The heart, as we would expect, is where our Lord is. We might say that the Holy Spirit is Jesus' *alter ego*. He who was with the first disciples in the flesh is with His contemporary disciples in the Spirit. This is a great mystery and it is beyond my ability to explain. What I understand is: to be in the spirit is to be in the divine presence. Remember how John of Revelation was *in the spirit* on the Lord's day? Because he was, he heard Jesus, who is *Alpha* and *Omega*, speak to him. Thus, the Holy Spirit is the agent of revelation, the same revelation that the disciples perceived in Jesus, "the faithful witness."

In hearing the living Word, John saw the exalted Jesus in the center of His Church: the creator, initiator of all things, and head of the body. As He had said to His disciples, "Lo, I am with you alway, even unto the end of the world" (Matt. 28:20), so He was saying to John, "I am he that liveth, and was dead; and, behold, I am alive for evermore" (Rev. 1:18). It is a glorious picture John paints of his living Lord present with him in the spirit.

I cannot say that I have had an experience exactly like that recorded in the Book of Revelation. By temperament I am not given to wild enthusiasms and great emotional highs. There is too much of the dour Scot about me. Yet, I think I understand what the John of Revelation is telling me. I have recorded in my book, *Through the Valley of the Kwai*, how I was ushered into the presence of the living Jesus by the faithfulness of a few men who loved me, by that "greater love," back to life. In doing so, they ushered me graciously into that living presence. At a Communion service in our jungle church, I experienced both the presence of our Lord, and the presence of the community of saints. This experience was shared by many others. Along with them I could have said, "I was in the spirit on the Lord's day."

This experience is repeated for me continuously in the celebration of the Holy Communion. At such moments I am conscious of my kinship with my Lord and His people. The great cloud of witnesses is all around me. I know I am one with all the dear and holy dead who are now at rest; and one with all my brethren in the spirit, including those in Africa, Britain, China, Russia and the islands of the seas. Should anyone challenge me to prove this, I would have to say, "I can't." Although I cannot, I have the certitude of the Presence who unites us with all the presences of the household of faith. As a celebrant in the act of Communion, I am very conscious of this. The gracious Words of Invitation, "Come unto me all ye that labor . . . ," the Bread which I break in the presence of the congregation; the Cup of the New Covenant which I raise for all to see; combine to open the door of that other dimension for me. In our Lord's presence, we are in the eternal because we are in the spirit.

The Paraclete promised by Jesus is "another Comforter" (John 14:16). One, that is, who teaches us to be strong in our faith. He does this by abiding with us, as Jesus promised, "that he may abide with you for ever" (John 14:16). He stands by us, that is, so that we are strengthened by His presence. When I was about fourteen, I rowed from my home on a rocky headland to an island five miles away to see a friend. I stayed too long. The day was ending. A storm blew up when I was about halfway home. The waves crashed over my bow. I could not stop to bail, otherwise I would be swept back by the wind. I became so exhausted that I felt I could not possibly make the last mile. In despair, I turned my head to take a last look at home. There, standing on the point, was my father. I was strengthened to keep going. In much the same sort of way, the Holy Spirit stands by us, not to coddle us, but to comfort, and this means He strengthens us. The eternal presence makes us strong, so strong that we may say with St. Paul, "I can do all things through Christ which strengtheneth me" (Phil. 4:13).

This is surely the victory of our faith: so to live in the divine presence that nothing can overcome our faith; not even death. Is not this the witness of the martyr?

In this presence we learn at first hand, through the teaching power of the Comforter, who is "the spirit of truth." Again we note how the work and influence of Jesus continues in the activity of the Holy Spirit. This teaching is centered in the revelation of the Word become flesh. Our Lord, as the "teacher come from God," was both the lesson and the teacher, the message and the messenger. Thus it is Jesus, and His teaching, that is the object of the Holy Spirit's instruction. "He shall teach you all things, and bring all things to your remembrance, whatsoever I have said unto you" (John 14:26).

We may imagine how the first disciples thought about Jesus and His words. I do not think they understood Him very well at first. They followed Him for many reasons, but chiefly, I think, because of His unique authority. It marked Him as different. At times He was so different from what they expected of the Messiah that they were puzzled by the difference. Gradually they were led to accept Him as the Messiah, the Son of the living God. Yet, even at this graduation point they did not understand in depth. For example, they did not understand that He had to go to Jerusalem to suffer many things, and to be executed. They did not understand that terrible execution, thus they fled. They did not understand the miracle of His resurrection, thus they went back to their fishing.

We could say they did not understand as a fellowship what their Lord had taught them until seven weeks after the Resurrection. Then they remembered! His teaching and His actions were all of one piece. Because they were, so were the disciples. No longer were they isolated as lonely individuals by their anxieties. They were one in the Spirit, one in the Lord. They had become the Spirit-filled community inspired to teach others of what God had done in the man Jesus. What are the Gospels but the remembrance of Jesus and His ways and words? What are the contemporary Christians but those who have been inspired by the Holy Spirit to say "Yes" to the Jesus of whom they have learned through the New Covenant, and the faithful word-bearing disciples who in turn became disciples because of the faithfulness of the first disciples? By the faith of a long line of disciples we are brought back to Jesus in the days of His earthly ministry.

You may be horrified to learn that I began to teach the gospel before I knew it. Three Australian soldiers came to see me, after I had turned from death to life in prison camp, to ask if I would teach them the Christian faith. I laughed at the request. Its sincerity, however, made me change my mind. I agreed to do my best. At the same time I warned my unknown "angels" that my teaching might turn them against Christianity. Their reply astonished me: "We don't care. It is either fair dinkum, or it is not. And if it is fair dinkum, we'll soon know." ("Fair dinkum" is an Australian slang phrase for truth.)

I had some knowledge of classical and Western philosophy and history. I am glad I had this background. But what made our learning experience "fair dinkum" was the Gospels. I was blessed in that I had no commentaries for reference. What I had were honest inquirers, the Gospels, and the Holy Spirit. When we studied the written Word together, it was transformed into the living Word. The life and words of Jesus became alive. His Sermon on the Mount became the standard by which we ought to live, the very dynamic of moral energy.

What I found personally was that my inward experiences of the mystery of grace were articulated by what I learned of Jesus. The more I learned, the more I loved Him. The more I loved Him, the more I loved my comrades. The more I loved my comrades, the more I loved my enemies. By loving my captors, they were no longer my enemies. They were my neighbors.

It was in this way that I learned that the Incarnate Word is the Word who *integrates* our inward experiences of grace so they become understandable. By this act of integration, the words spoken by Jesus, and preserved in the Gospels, are *interpreted* for us. We are

241

now in that happy position of knowing the truth. The
eyes of our faith are opened to see God. Yes, to see God.
For this is what Jesus promised: "He that hath seen me
hath seen the Father" (John 14:9).

There are times when I look back wistfully on that
teaching experience. It was a time of light and joy: a
time when we were one in the spirit. The gospel came
to us in a death camp as the Word of life. Perhaps it
was easy then: for the difference that Jesus is, and
makes, was brilliantly clear. He alone could speak to
our condition. What I have found in the institutional
church is that too many people trust commentaries
and commentators too much, and the Holy Spirit too
little. Human reason can never build a stairway to
heaven. We are always dependent upon the revealing
act of God whereby He makes himself known to us.
Only upon the foundation of revelation may we build
the structures of our theologies. If the foundation is not
there, the structures will crumble.

We may speak of a continuing revelation because the
Holy Spirit is continuously revealing Jesus as Lord to
us. This revelation occurs in the experience of every
believer in every generation. That is why people like
myself have to realize that this revelation, which is
claimed by me for myself, is the same revelation
granted to the first disciples, and to every disciple,
regardless of time, place and civilization.

I like St. Paul's description of this truth in Galatians
3:23-29: "Before faith came, we were kept under the
law, shut up unto the faith which should afterwards be
revealed. Wherefore the law was our schoolmaster to
bring us unto Christ, that we might be justified by
faith. But after that faith is come, we are no longer
under a schoolmaster. For ye are all the children of
God by faith in Christ Jesus. For as many of you as have

been baptized into Christ have put on Christ. There is neither Jew nor Greek, there is neither bond nor free, there is neither male nor female: for ye are all one in Christ Jesus. And if ye be Christ's, then are ye Abraham's seed, and heirs according to the promise."

All are one everywhere, in every time, in every way, through the teaching work of the Holy Spirit who fulfills the work Jesus described, "he shall testify of me" (John 15:26).

St. John goes on to tell us that the Holy Spirit is at work in the world as well as within us. We are not left to our own devices. We are not solely responsible for the world's salvation. Sometimes we think we are. When we do, we become dispirited, anxious, bitter and self-righteous. Once when I saw a Christian student looking very unhappy, I asked him what was the trouble. He replied, "I'm no good. I've prayed and prayed and nothing has happened. The Holy Spirit has abandoned me."

"What are you praying for?" I asked.

"The souls of my roommates. There are five of them. We're in a big suite. I prayed that God would use me to convert them before the end of the month. The month is over. Everything is the same. Nothing has happened. I've failed. God doesn't want me."

"Don't be daft," I told him. "You're testing God. You're telling Him what to do, and when. I pray every day for the salvation of this university, and this country, and this world. I can't do it. Only God can, in His way, and in His time. My prayer is: Father, your shoulders are broader than mine. If you can't carry the world's burdens, I can't. Help me to be faithful, and available."

My troubled friend probably thought I was a man of little faith, as I may be, for he shuffled off with a pained look in his eyes. All I was trying to tell him was that it is God who gives the increase. Jesus has described what the Holy Spirit is doing, "He will reprove the world of sin, and of righteousness, and of judgment" (John 16:8). This He seems to be doing in the half an hour I've described as the *eschaton*-point.

I hope I have said enough, if barely enough, to suggest our dependence upon the guidance of the Holy Spirit. Where He is, there is Christ. Where Christ is, there is the fullness of the godhead bodily. Never allow anyone to tempt you to think that the Holy Spirit and Jesus the Christ are separate, so separate that the power of Christ is one thing, and the power of the Holy Spirit another. They are both the visible and invisible action of the revealing Father. I take it that this is what St. Paul meant when he wrote to the church in Colossae saying, "For it pleased the Father that in him should all the fulness dwell" (Col. 1:19). That "in him" is, of course, Jesus.

The more I think about it, the more I realize that this growing up in the spirit is an endless experience precisely because it is in the spirit. It is eternal. The eternal is endless: it is eternally open for life. It has no end; no terminus. It is in our experience, and, therefore, in space and time. Yet it is beyond our experience. The open door is the man Jesus, who is the way, and as the way is the resurrection and the life. This life we share with Him by faith.

This makes me optimistic about existence. It is not an end, but a preparation: the schoolroom in which we learn of God first-hand through the mediation of our Lord, and the inspiration of the Holy Spirit. From whom could we learn the truth but from the source of truth?

This brings us back again to the reality of God's

revelation of himself in the flesh, and in the spirit. As the spirit pointed forward to the revelation in the flesh, so the spirit today points back to it. It is the centering point of time and eternity. It gives us direction for the past and for the future. It gives us the saving event to think about. We look backward and forward at the same time in trust and in hope. Our salvation, which is eternal, is in space and time. We have the evidence. That is why we may say with the confidence of St. Paul, "For I have received of the Lord that which I also delivered unto you" (1 Cor. 11:23). Our lives are based on this fact, and not on an illusion. Thus, our faith has a firm foundation on which to grow. The evidence of things unseen has a tangible source. The unseen is visible.

As I write this, I realize how difficult it is for most people to accept such teaching. At the first time round, it sounds meaningless. At the second time round, it sounds crazy. It is all about invisible, inward growth. We are conditioned not to believe in it.

What do we truly believe in as individuals and as a nation? Is it not physical growth that may be measured by the bank balance, or by the number of cars, electric typewriters, hi-fi systems, TV sets and a thousand useless gadgets? Did not Jesus speak unkindly about the person who perceives growth in this way? "Thou fool, this night thy soul shall be required of thee" (Luke 12:20).

What is a person if he or she has only grown rich, or powerful, or famous? Such growth may merit an important, expensive funeral. That is all!

The inward maturing of the spirit is a growing into life. When we talk about truth as Christians, we are not talking about 2 x 2, but about the truth by which we live, the truth which sets us free. This truth is not an abstraction. It is Jesus! Was not this why He told

His disciples in the Upper Room, "I am the way, the truth, and the life" (John 14:6)? Compare this statement with the revelation granted to Moses at Horeb: "I am that I am" (Exod. 3:14). This truth may only be known at first-hand. And who may help us attain this goal but the Holy Spirit?

The way to maturity

We grow up in the Presence by learning from him first-hand. We thank our tutors for taking us this far, bid them farewell, and accept the responsibility for the salvation given to us.

To mature in the spirit thus means that we learn to take ourselves seriously because we have taken God seriously. It is rather like growing up in a loving family. The atmosphere is one where the child learns to trust herself because she knows she can trust her father and her mother. She learns to love because she is loved. This education is more a matter of presence than of rules. She learns to be an authentic person from those who are authentically personal. The characteristic of personhood, as I understand it, is freedom.

People who have never been permitted to exercise their individual freedom tend to be either overly submissive or overly rebellious. When carried to extreme, these qualities become destructive. The means of growth are frustrated, and the soul is kept on ice.

Spiritual development implies a basic personal freedom. This freedom, in turn, implies struggling, striving and suffering. Our growth in freedom is one of action, interaction and reaction. This is the dialectic of personal life. We have the freedom to wrestle with God and the problems of existence. In such a striving, our *egos* are braised. Regardless of what popular gurus may say, the spiritual life is not easy. It is not easy to be different as Jesus was different. It is not easy to realize our authentic freedom within our family, or peer group, or society. It is not easy to affirm the divine righteousness we know by faith, and to say as so many martyrs have done, "Here I stand. I can do no other." To say this is to affirm one's God-given freedom; that which grace makes possible.

Those of you who are familiar with the writings of Dietrich Bonhoeffer will recall how he reminded members of the confessing church of Germany that grace and freedom are costly. His sacrificial living in the Germany of World War II and his execution by the Nazis, demonstrated this teaching. In his poem, "Stations on the Way to Freedom," he mentions four stations. These are:

1. *Discipline*, which means the mastery of the Christ-centered will over sense and soul.

2. *Action*, which is doing the gospel. This involves us in doing what is right, but not popular. It thrusts us into "the tempest of living."

3. *Suffering*, which comes from yielding our freedom to God to be perfected in glory.

4. *Death;* the nature of Christian freedom is that it faces and accepts death. Our acceptance is liberating. This is in contrast with the expectations of secular societies which affirm happiness as the supreme good. By such an affirmation, they refuse to accept death. In the light, therefore, of Christian freedom we can see why the martyrs have been so conscious of eternal life that they were unconcerned about their prospects of temporal happiness. My way of expressing this is that they were so sure of life that they willingly walked on the boundaries of death.

Maturing in Freedom

I believe that the meaning of personal freedom is rooted in the Bible. We could say this is what the biblical faith is all about. It is the characteristic of the relationship between God and His people. By the act of creation, God set the cosmos free to be itself. By the creation of man/woman as a living soul, God set him/her free to respond to the divine call to fellowship. So great is the range of this freedom that we may conclude we are free to choose the bliss of heaven with our Lord, or the torment of hell without Him. Such a conclusion emphasizes not only the uniqueness, but the awful seriousness of this freedom.

When God revealed himself to Moses on Mount Sinai, He prefaced the giving of the Decalogue with these words: "I am the Lord thy God, which have brought thee out of the land of Egypt, out of the house of bondage" (Exod. 20:2). Another translation is: "I am the Lord your God who brought you out of the land of Egypt and its prison camps."

The message of the literary prophets is one which called the people of Israel to their freedom in God. The Israelites were the witnesses of this freedom to the rest of the world. A splendid statement to this effect is to be found in Isaiah 41.

The revelation of Jesus, however, takes us to the ultimate understanding of personal freedom. The story of the New Testament is that of the freest of men who set others free. We see this truth in the account of Jesus' visit to his village of Nazareth immediately after His temptations. On the Sabbath He read the lesson in the synagogue from Isaiah 61. He stated that He was the fulfiller of the prophecy. Thus, we learn, He is the Anointed One sent by God to announce good news to the poor, to proclaim the release of prisoners, to recover sight for the blind, to grant freedom for the broken victims of existence, and to proclaim the Lord's time of favor and salvation (Luke 4:18, 19).

He made it clear to His fellow villagers that the liberation promised by God to Israel was now in effect. The members of the synagogue became infuriated when they realized that He claimed to be their Messiah. They forced Him to leave the village and tried to hurl Him over a cliff. But His hour had not yet come so He passed through the angry crowd to continue His witness elsewhere.

The picture Luke gives us is that of the divine/human liberator who has come to set His people free. His freedom was not economic, political, academic, nor individual, but divine. We may say that the reign of God, which He initiated, is the reign of God's freedom: the evidence of the divine love. When Calvinists used the much misunderstood word *predestination*, they did so to affirm that salvation is the work of grace; and that our true freedom is within God's freedom. By the revealing Word, we are called into freedom.

Freedom in the spirit is our experience of grace: for by it we are set free from the bondage of sin, fear and guilt. It is this freedom in grace that provides the atmosphere and *ethos* in which we mature as God's children.

By our study of God's story of redemption in the Gospels, we learn how Jesus' ministry was one of liberation. From the cradle to the cross, He set His people free. By faith, we participate in the benefits of His work. This is simply another way of saying we share in the life of His resurrection as He promised: "Whosoever liveth and believeth in me shall never die" (John 11:26). We also learn how those who were set free rejoiced in their freedom. What do we do in our divinely given freedom? We give thanks, of course! Is not this what St. Paul told the Philippians? "Rejoice in the Lord alway: and again I say, Rejoice" (Phil. 4:4). We present our bodies as "a living sacrifice" (Rom. 12:1).

Freedom is a miracle in the universe, and the greatest miracle of all is the turning from the destructive freedom of rebellion against God to the creative freedom, which is that of loving Him and our neighbors.

Our understanding of freedom is nurtured by our study of the Bible. We have noted that God set His creation free by the act of creation. It was set free to be itself. Any author or artist understands a little of what this means. When she or he completes a work, it is released from the artist's vision, imagination and faith to be itself in its own right. Although it is independent of its creator, it is nevertheless his creation. Because it is, he continues to care for it. In the human realm we, who have been created, claim our autonomy without reference to our origin, and thereby participate in the Fall.

Our affirmation of independence leads to disorder, destruction and death. This is the human story. The divine story is, however, that we have been redeemed, or re-created by God's saving act in Jesus. This task of re-creation continues in our life through the work of the Holy Spirit.

The way to maturity, therefore, is the way of freedom. It is in this freedom, and because of it, that we grow. Not, however, in our own likeness, but in the likeness of Him who sets us free. We are set free to be God's children, which means we are free to be like God. This, surely, is what our kinship with Him means.

The way of freedom is, however, the way of the cross. This means: *Crisis Existence*. We may characterize this as a mark of discipleship. We cannot be a disciple unless we bear our own cross (Luke 14:27). Jesus said this *before* His crucifixion. Remarkable, is it not, that He should have used this symbol of infamy as the mark of our kinship with Him at that time?

It is the cost of freedom. To bear our cross is to live in crisis, that is to make decisions and judgments which may separate us from others, and all that we may have held dear before meeting the Jesus of the cross.

In our freedom we make our decision for Him. Every decision we make afterwards is influenced and shaped by this essential one. Once having made it, we keep on making it. We participate continuously in a spiritual lesson. The problem we are left to solve is the problem of ourselves, our relationships and our priorities. Each time we face the crisis of making our decision for Jesus Christ instead of for family, friends, peer group, we are strengthened to be more Christ-like and, therefore, more mature.

St. Peter, remember, was challenged three times by the risen Christ: "Simon, son of Jonas, lovest thou me more than these?" (John 21:15). What is termed the once-and-for-all decision is in fact the decision we are required to make in times of crises. Jesus or mammon; Jesus or the libido; Jesus or Karl Marx; Jesus or public opinion? There is no compromise.

Marks of Maturity

There are many. I mention but a few, beginning with one that is so important for those who are engaged in the life of the mind.

1. *Our vocation as students or scholars is to be holy.*

Our reason is evil just as our bodies are evil with their desires. It may only be redeemed by the action of grace, along with our response to it in the form of

251

obedience. This obedience involves us in what we may think of as intellectual holiness. I define this as thinking within the dimension of grace, and within the tutelage of faith. Our faculties exist as servants of God. As such they may be used by Him in His creative and reconciling ways.

But how do we achieve this? The answer has already been indicated. It may be summed up best in St. Paul's statement: "If so be that ye have heard him, and have been taught by him, as the truth is in Jesus: That ye put off concerning the former conversation the old man, which is corrupt according to the deceitful lusts; And be renewed in the spirit of your mind; And that ye put on the new man, which after God is created in righteousness and true holiness" (Eph. 4:21-24).

Justification by faith implies the salvation of the mind, which as experience shows along with the Bible is just as prideful, if not more so, as our other faculties.

St. Paul also tells us to have the mind of Christ (Phil. 2:5). He tells us what this means: humility. It is the way of the cross. It is through the obedient and humble mind that God's people perceive new intellectual possibilities, as well as discerning the wisdom inherited from the past. It is by this humility that honest dialogue is initiated, and continued as a means of opening this personal communication to the gospel. It is also by this humility of mind that we continue our learning and our thinking, knowing that there is no salvation in them.

The more we think with the humble mind, the more we learn of God's ways and wonders. In doing so, we become more integrated as whole personalities who are being re-created in the image of Christ. According to my understanding of recent scientific thought, science is beginning to learn from the wisdom of the Bible. The mind and the brain, faith and reason, the heart and the mind are one. It is in this way that the Bible speaks of the heart and the mind. "Create in me a clean heart, O God" (Ps. 51:10). And, "Be ye transformed by the renewing of your mind" (Rom. 12:2). Heart and mind are obviously interchangeable terms.

2. *Our lives are to reveal the orderliness of grace.*
These lines of John Greenleaf Whittier (1807-1892) express what I mean:

And let our ordered lives confess
The beauty of thy peace.

They speak of the calm after the storm, and the peace after the conflict. It is this kind of order that marks the Christian as mature. Crisis-existence is never easy. It is, however, the atmosphere in which we grow up through tension and conflict. St. Paul is a glorious example of the ordered life. Think, for example, of his final exhortation to the divided church of Galatia: "From henceforth let no man trouble me: for I bear in my body the marks of the Lord Jesus" (Gal. 6:17). This was his last argument against those who taught that physical circumcision was essential for church membership. St. Paul's statement is a "not so" one. The marks are the wounds of faithfulness: scars for Christ. As such, they are the evidence of the person whose life is orderly because it is centered in Christ.

It is fairly obvious that everyday human existence cannot be maintained effectively without some kind of basic order. A disordered home is slovenly, dirty, disoriented and confusing. We may object, in our childhood, to our mothers when they ask us to drop our toys in order to eat the meal they have prepared. But when we grow up we like to have our meals hot at regular times. In much the same way we may think our parents unduly fussy because they want us to act in a moral way. But as we grow older we appreciate the fact that our parents were teaching us the art of living with each other. We may have complained at one time about the family insistence upon good manners only to discover later on that we were being taught the discipline of caring for one another. Good manners are, after all, simply an expression of orderly living.

Our education does not occur in chaos. It could not, because it is basically an orderly way of understanding and interpreting the universe in which we exist, and those with whom we live. There is no meaning or understanding in chaos.

Colleagues in European universities have told me of the distress they experienced while teaching in universities characterized by the label "free." This label means that the university is free from the Christian faith and ethics, and free for Marxist interpretation. This way was characterized by Aleksandr Solzhenitsyn as the way of disorder in his Harvard address of June, 1978. We have seen, in the first four chapters of this book, that secular humanism tried to locate order in the human realm without reference to God. As a Godless faith, its fruits were consequently disorder, despair and destruction. This, too, is Solzhenitsyn's point: "As humanism in its development became more and more materialistic, it made itself increasingly accessible to speculation and manipulation, at first by socialism and then by communism. So that Karl Marx was able to say in 1844 that 'communism is naturalized humanism.'"

Once again it is to the recorded revelation of God in the Bible that we must turn for direction. According to the account of creation, it is God who gave order to the earth that was formless and chaotic. The word "void" is used in the English translation to indicate emptiness, desolation, nothingness. Creation, therefore, was the divine act of giving form, meaning, order to this nothingness.

In the light of this interpretation, we see that sin results in disorder: for this is what disobedience is all about. The further we go from God, the closer we come to that primordial chaos which is the habitat of Satan.

The work of Jesus was that of reconciling the world unto His Father (2 Cor. 5:18). To reconcile is to bring together in an orderly way that which was separated, divided, polarized and chaotic. When two people are in violent disagreement with each other, they may go to the absurd limit of fighting each other to the death. When two enemies are reconciled, they enter into a new relationship with each other, one that is obviously an improvement upon the earlier one of disorder.

Our Lord's sacrifice upon the cross is the saving act which transforms our human disorder by initiating the new order of redemption and grace. Thus, by faith we participate in this new order.

I have written earlier of our human existence taking place within sight of the *eschaton*-point and the *eschaton*-person. This is simply a Christian way of saying that our human pride brings our civilizations to judgment and chaos, and that the work of our Lord brings us to salvation. We may say that Christian ethics is eschatological because we live by faith in the divinely initiated moral order of *agape,* that is, divine love. As the end of time is time's redemption, so the end of pride through repentance is the beginning of new life in the eternal order. This is the order, therefore, that "our ordered lives confess."

The truth of this great hope and affirmation is made brilliantly clear in these words of our Lord: "Now is the judgment of this world, now shall the ruler of this world be cast out; and I, when I am lifted up from the earth, will draw all men to myself" (John 12:31, 32 RSV). Thus, this world, and its satanic ruler, have been judged and cast out into the chaos, or disorder, of which it and he are part. At the same time, everyone everywhere is drawn or attracted to the crucified Savior who reigns in glory. He is the divine center, and, therefore, the creator of moral and spiritual order.

By the act of conversion, we turn to Him to look upon the profound love of God. Thereafter our lives are renewed by His presence as the Holy Spirit. In His presence our lives are given order and meaning, and we are thereby saved from the hell of nothingness and chaos. Once again I must refer to St. Paul's description of the order Jesus creates: "The whole universe has been created through him and for him. And he exists before everything, and all things are held together in him. He is, moreover, the head of the body, the church" (Col. 1:16-18 NEB).

This superb definition of our Lord's being and activity tells us of the ordered life. It is not the result of social conditioning, negative and positive, but the divine gift bestowed upon us by the act of creation, and the act of redemption.

These two acts are the ground of the moral order in St. Paul's letters. When he gives his practical advice, he begins with the acceptable forms of social order practiced by Jews according to the teaching of the synagogues. From there he goes on to show the fulfillment of this order within the New Covenant. The disorder of the Corinthian Church, which was due to an immature faith, was to be overcome by doing everything "decently and in order" (1 Cor. 14:40). The meaning of "decently and in order" is carefully spelled out in the previous chapter, the chapter on *agape*.

It is in this light that we are to understand the meaning of Romans 13. The first seven verses deal with the natural order of creation. The remaining verses refer to the completion of this order through Christ's work. Thus, St. Paul writes, "Owe no man any thing, but to love one another: for he that loveth another hath fulfilled the law" (Rom. 13:8). His summing up is contained in these words, "But put ye on the Lord Jesus Christ" (Rom. 13:14).

Putting on Christ, and being in Christ refer surely to the reality of centering our lives upon Him, and thereby revealing the Person we love above everyone else; and in whose ordering of life we choose to live. By so doing, we reflect, "The beauty of thy peace."

When we see this beauty in the lives of others, we are introduced, or reminded, of the beauty of the Father shining on the face of Jesus Christ.

I have written that the marks of the ordered life show the scars of Christ. In doing so I am recognizing the reality of our experiences in this world. The chaos of this world disturbs us, even to the extent of causing us to be depressed. Perhaps such depression is inevitable. It is due to our experience of disorder in society, in ourselves and in our bodies. We experience the disorder in terms of violence, aggression, indifference, insensitivity, competition, rejection. We know our own inner disorder of fear, jealousy, bitterness, hatred, indecision, ambivalence, insecurity. The chemistry of our body is not perfect. Its imbalance is due to improper nutrition; too high a concentration of metal tracents such as copper, lead and aluminum; or the improper use of drugs.

Experiences of these and other forms of depression

are evidences of our creatureliness. They are common to us all. In reading Psalms, I have noted how often the Psalmist complains of depression. A few that come to mind are: 18, 22, 35, 39, 42, 51, 69, 70, 88, 137, 142, 143. These, and others you may think of, speak of this common experience. They also speak, however, of the joy that transcends depression because God is the one we worship and serve. The metaphors for God in the Psalms focus our attention upon His otherness, His objective reality, His ultimate authority. Thus we have metaphors such as Shepherd, Rock, Fortress, Buckler, Horn of Salvation, High Tower and Deliverer. These tell us of the life ordered in, upon and through God.

The New Testament tells us of the full revelation of God in Jesus. Everything is centered in Him, and founded upon Him. In Him, and through Him, we have order, meaning and purpose. What is more, we have the victory. This is what our Lord says: "These things I have spoken unto you, that in me ye might have peace. In the world ye shall have tribulation: but be of good cheer; I have overcome the world" (John 16:33).

3. *The third mark of maturity is simply that of Church membership.* To be in Christ is to be in His Body, the Church. I cannot conceive of the witness of the individual Christian without the witness of the whole Church. Both belong together like head and tails on the same coin. The ordered life we are to live is within the ordered life of Christ's Body.

My impression is that much of contemporary American church life is more a witness to its immaturity than to its maturity in Christ. Individual pride fragments the Church. To paraphrase George Orwell's phrase in *Animal Farm*, "While all Christians are equal, some are more equal than others." Those who

are more equal are generally those who think they
know more than other Christians, or know better, or
are better, or are more elect, or are more selective.
Thus they say along with the more equal Corinthians:
"I am of Paul"; "I am of Apollos"; "I am of Cephas"; "I
am of Rome"; "I am of Canterbury"; "I am of Luther";
"I am of Calvin"; "I am Fundamentalist"; "I am
Liberal"; "I am Charismatic"; "I am a Bible believer."
Should not we all be saying, "Jesus is Lord"? And how
can we say that Jesus is Lord if it is not in the power of
the Holy Spirit (1 Cor. 12:3)? And if we say Jesus is
Lord, does not this mean that we are one and equal
with everyone who says it? We are the Body of Christ,
and members in particular (1 Cor. 12:27). Our Lord
has chosen, and appointed, one Body to be His voice,
hands and feet in the world. As I have indicated in
chapter five much of the ineffectiveness of Christians
on campuses is due to their inability to witness as one
body. What miracles will happen when we all ". . .
stand firm in one spirit, with one mind striving side by
side for the faith of the gospel, and not frightened in
anything by [our] opponents" (Phil. 1:27 RSV).

So inseparable is the individual from the Church
that the Letter to the Ephesians tells us that, "Now, in
Christ Jesus ye who sometimes were far off are made
nigh by the blood of Christ. For he is our peace, who
hath made both one, and hath broken down the middle
wall of partition between us; having abolished in his
flesh the enmity, even the law of commandments contained in ordinances; for to make in himself of twain
one new man, so making peace" (Eph. 2:13, 14). Note,
by the way, that "one new man." Does not this mean
that although we are many, we are one? Because we
are one, we are therefore bound to seek out one another.
This we may do by presenting our bodies at an eleven

o'clock service on a Sunday morning wherever we may be; and by joining our witness to that of others at times of moral crisis. As I said earlier, when two or three gather together in the Lord's presence there is every likelihood that four or five will tag along as well. How many were there at Pentecost? Eleven old disciples, and one new one. Pentecost was an event that shook the world. Twelve men were one, but their power was infinite. We understand why: because ". . . they were all with one accord in one place" (Acts 2:1). Their hearts and minds were one. They were "one new man." Thus, the world could not stop them.

Church membership is not a subscription to a club, but a commitment to Jesus Christ and His kinsfolk. As I have indicated earlier, the power of the Spirit-filled fellowship is infinite. Because of it miracles happen. One of the greatest of these in our secular society and its universities is the miracle of faith.

The miracle of faith means the miracle of truth. To be *in Christ* is to be in His truth. It alone can set us free. This results in the fellowship of joy. This is the work of Christ. He has overcome the world (John 16:33). Our joy is in the fellowship of those who share Christ's suffering in the world. St. Paul's letter to his beloved kinsfolk in Philippi was written shortly before his execution. What does he say? He says, "Rejoice in the Lord alway: and again I say Rejoice" (Phil. 4:4). This is the response of the whole Church to their Lord who is with them.

This characteristic of joy in fellowship is the mark of our maturity. While others moan and complain about God's unfairness to them, we sing His praise. We do so because He has given us a new song to sing in a strange land. It is the personal evidence of the faith that prevails set in the midst of the faith that fails.

Faith is God's gift to everyone. It is the characteristic of our creatureliness. We do not manufacture it. On the contrary, it is what we are by the divine act of creation. Creation, however, is only completed by redemption, and by redemption we mean the whole saving act of God in Jesus. Every human being has faith. Salvation is not in faith itself, but in its object. Saving faith is faith in Jesus through whom God has revealed himself in the flesh.

What I mean by the faith that fails is simply faith centered upon itself, human existence and the dimension of physical phenomena. Secular humanism is an incompleted faith. It is the prideful faith of those who believe reality may be reduced to atoms, matter in motion, or mathematical and socio/political formulas. Contemporary history records the grim failure of such an inadequate faith. The evidence of this faith is harshly manifested in fascism, Nazism, communism and most of the other "isms," as well as in Jonestown, bruised and broken babies, tyrannical bureaucracies and wars. This inadequate faith is too small and limiting for human well-being and fulfillment. The environment it creates brings about the death of the soul. Jesus referred to this when He warned His disciples not to be afraid of those who could kill the body. They were to be afraid instead of those who had the power to bring about the soul's death. Perhaps we may refer to this power as the field of reference and meaning. The physical field is that of laws which enable us to think about the physical universe. Such a field is too confining for the maturing of our souls. We need a bigger field: one that is eternal.

This "field" of eternal significance is similar to the principle of homeostasis known to ecologists. A homeostatic system is one which is directed or oriented toward an end. This end, or goal, provides stability and continuity. W.B. Cannon, of Cambridge, Massachusetts, used this word "homeostasis" in 1932 to illustrate how a constant composition of the blood is maintained in mammals regardless of the changes that occur in their immediate environment. This stability ensures the continuity of the species. The spiritual homeostasis is one which has Christ as its end. Through Him we have life, continuing and eternal. He provides us with the homeostasis essential for life and its many expressions. In simpler words, faith in Him is the faith that prevails. By faith our wills are centered in Him to the extent that we may speak as St. Paul does of *being in Christ*. Through Him we have our stability and identity. Because we have, we are thus free to encourage and reinforce this same quality in our brothers and sisters in the fellowship of faith.

The homeostasis thus initiated by God's action in creation and redemption grants us our stability as authentic persons, or children of God. It is one of relationship: the relationship of love by which God brings us into His presence. His presence, or living Word, gives us our field of reference and meaning. What we see in secular humanism is the defection from, and rejection of, this creative, lively homeostasis. The movement is away from God to humanity, which simply means the idea about human beings; to the dimension of observable phenomena; to the disregard of human beings; to technocracy and its multiple bureaucracies; to anarchy, revolution and tyranny. Many of the values used by secular humanism are stolen without awareness from Christian humanism, which exalts people by giving them their rightful place. Where is that? In the presence of God. What is Marxist communism, by the way, but an attempt to secularize Jesus' teachings on the kingdom of God?

Secular humanism is the faith that fails. It is, alas, the faith that dominates in too many areas of our Western civilization. When Winston Churchill assumed office as Prime Minister of the United Kingdom in the spring of 1940, he reminded Great Britain that the war against Germany was a war for the preservation of a Christian civilization. Although too few in the West are conscious of this today, this conflict still continues. The Christian faith has prevailed for nearly 2,000 years. To this we may add another 2,000 years to include Abraham as our ancestor: for so far as our human awareness is concerned the community of faith begins with Him, and is completed through Jesus. We have the certitude that it will prevail. The task of Christ's Church is to welcome people everywhere into the community of faith where He reigns at the center in the love that prevails.

In light of secular humanism, our challenge is one which calls us to do the following:

1. To get our priorities straight. This may mean abandoning our pet neuroses and intellectual hang-ups in order to let Jesus be Lord of our individual and corporate lives, both in the Church and in our civilization.

2. To be obedient to Jesus as Lord. Submission to Him does not mean enslavement, but freedom: freedom to say *NO* to the principalities and powers of this world, and *YES* to Jesus and His reign of victorious love.

3. To be armed for the continuing conflict against the hosts of the devil in every area of our existence. St. Paul in his sixth chapter of the letter to the Ephesians tells us how to stand fast and endure by:

a. having girded our loins with truth;

b. having put on the breast plate of righteousness;

c. having shod our feet with the sandals of peace;

d. having taken up the great shield of faith;

e. wearing the helmet of salvation; and by,

f. strapping on the sword of the Holy Spirit, and using it to discern between truth and lies.

The holy war has continued, and will continue, until God's end is completed in His way, and in His time (*kairos*). In every generation there are many battle-fields. None is more important than that of the university campus. It is not a neutral no-man's-land; it is either the Lord's or the devil's. So far as students are concerned this means it is either the place of their bondage, or of their freedom: that freedom to which St. Paul witnesses, ". . . where the Spirit of the Lord is, there is liberty" (2 Cor. 3:17).